morning
B.R.E.W.

morning
B.R.E.W.

A Divine Power Drink for Your Soul

Kirk Byron Jones

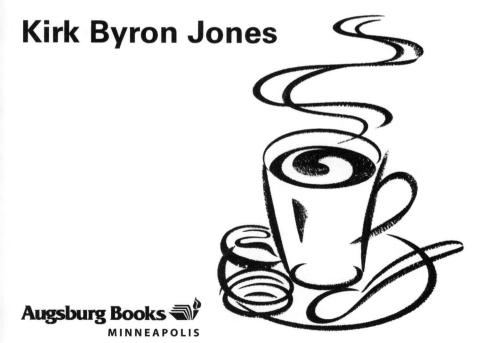

Augsburg Books
MINNEAPOLIS

To Markeithia Silver, my sister by loving choice. Markeithia, your spirit leapt the moment you first heard about Morning B.R.E.W. *In that instant, I knew this book needed to and would become a reality. Thank You.*

MORNING B.R.E.W.
A Divine Power Drink for Your Soul

Large-quantity purchases or custom editions of this book are available at a discount from the publisher. For more information, contact the sales department at Augsburg Fortress, Publishers, 1-800-328-4648, or write to: Sales Director, Augsburg Fortress, Publishers, P. O. Box 1209, Minneapolis, MN 55440-1209.

Scripture passages are from the New Revised Standard Version of the Bible, copyright © 1946, 1952, 1971, 1989 by the Division of Christian Education of the National Council of the Churches of Christ in the USA. Used by permission.

Library of Congress Cataloging-in-Publication Data
Jones, Kirk Byron.
   Morning B.R.E.W. : a divine power drink for your soul / Kirk Byron Jones.
      p. cm.
   ISBN 0-8066-5138-5 (pbk. : alk. paper)
   1. Devotion. 2. Devotional exercises. I. Title: Morning BREW. II. Title.
   BV4815.J66 2005
   248.3—dc22   2005007930

Cover design by Laurie Ingram; cover art © Illustration Works. Used by permission.
Book design by Michelle L. N. Cook

The paper used in this publication meets the minimum requirements of American National Standard for Information Sciences—Permanence of Paper for Printed Library Materials, ANSI Z329.48-1984. ♾™

Printed in Canada

09   08   07   06   05   1   2   3   4   5   6   7   8   9   10

Contents

Acknowledgments

My deepest gratitude and appreciation to Augsburg Fortress, Publishers, for catching the B.R.E.W. vision and being excited about it. I am especially grateful to Beth L. Lewis, President and CEO, for urging me to send my proposal for consideration. From proposal to final manuscript, many wonderful persons contributed their time and talent to the B.R.E.W. project. An extra-special thank you to Scott Tunseth, Lois Wallentine, Pamela Johnson, Bob Todd, and Michelle L. N. Cook. It was a joy working with you all. Now, get ready, more B.R.E.W. is on the way!

I am joyfully grateful for a holy wealth of family and friends. Thank you all for inspiring me in open and hidden ways, especially my merry-making spouse of nearly twenty-five years, Bunnie, and our fabulous offspring, Jasmine, Jared, Joya, and Jovonna.

Finally and fully, love to The Loving Mystery, God in Christ, who inspires my soul searching and satisfaction!

Definitions

Brew

The ancestral meaning of brew has basically to do with "heat." It comes from an Indo-European base of *bhreu-* or *bhru-*, which is also the source of the Latin *fervere* "boil," from which we get *fervent, ferment,* and the second syllable of *comfrey. Broth* and possibly *bread* can be traced back to the same Indo-European base, and some etymologists have linked it with *burn.*

—*Dictionary of Word Origins*, John Ayto

Morning B.R.E.W.

A five-to-thirty-minute morning ritual in which one creates and consumes a soulfully warming experience of *stillness, divine love, personal affirmation*, and *fresh living vitality.*

—Kirk Byron Jones

The Question

*Why shouldn't you
look forward
to each
new day,
and live
as many days
as you can
with as much
desire,
energy,
and passion
as you can?*
—K.B.J.

1. "I WAKED UP!"

"O Lord, in the morning you hear my voice; in the morning I plead my case to you, and watch."
—Psalm 5:3

"I will also give the morning star."
—Revelation 2:28

"Morning by morning new mercies, I see."
—Thomas O. Chisholm

"In the morning when I rise, give me Jesus."
—Negro Spiritual

A Child's Declaration

He did it for several weeks when he was three or four years old. Our son, Jared, now nineteen and in his first year of college, started waking up in an unusual fashion. To this day, we do not know what triggered it or what stopped it. During this time, his morning declaration alerted us to the beginning of each new day: "I waked up!" Sometimes he would shout it before we were ready to hear it: "I waked up!" He said it as if waking up was an event. After a few days, I wondered if something was wrong with him.

"Honey," I said to my wife, Bunnie, "Maybe we need to have him checked out."

Eventually the morning declaration ceased. Jared, however, remains a morning person to this day. Though he stopped saying, "I waked up!" the phrase took residence inside of me. At various moments in my life, Jared's morning decree would come back to me, not as a faint echo, but insatiably fresh and new. It reached a zenith pitch seven years ago, when I began to observing the first moments of each new day.

How did you wake up this morning? By that I mean, what were your first feelings, thoughts, and actions? How do you usually wake up? What are your usual first feelings, thoughts, and actions?

About seven years ago, for reasons I do not remember, I began studying my attitude and disposition upon waking up. I became intensely interested in "the me" that was coming into each new day. I began thinking about Jared's experience more deeply. It dawned on me that Jared was waking up twice each morning. The first time was an automatic physiological coming to awareness, the stirring that we all do as the body moves from rest to conscious engagement. This first awakening is an involuntary response to bodily stimuli. But Jared was waking up a second time. "I waked up!" was more of a voluntary, purposeful second awakening made in response to the first. Filled with gratitude that he could not explain, Jared chose to greet each day with enthusiastic acceptance. What could not be explained was, nonetheless, acclaimed with wondrous awe.

We all wake up twice. While the second awakening may be dependant on the first, it is in many ways the more important awakening. And it is the one that we have tremendous influence over. To prove that you have such power, try the following five-minute, two-step exercise. Tomorrow when you wake up (or after your next nap) take a moment to notice your initial feelings and thoughts upon waking. For the purposes of this exercise, do not analyze your feelings and thoughts; simply identify them in your mind. You may name your feelings and thoughts silently or out loud. After a couple of minutes, identify one or two positive thoughts to focus on. These positive thoughts may be thoughts that were already in the mix you previously identified or new thoughts. It does not matter. The point of this second step is to focus some of your formidable mental energy on these one or two positive thoughts, rolling them around in your mind, expanding them, feeding them, questioning them, and affirming them. Take no more than five minutes to attend to your original thoughts and focus on a couple of selected thoughts.

If you are not filled with overflowing positive energy after this brief exercise, do not worry; that is not the intent. The goal is to make you aware of your power to register and regulate your thinking. Such power may be at its height during your early waking moments, when mind and spirit are most rested and ready for fresh awareness and new engagement.

The ability to register and regulate your thinking, which involves both imagination and rationale is the most powerful ability you have. We are admonished in the Bible to be transformed by the renewing of our minds (Romans 12:2).

We are told that persons are as they think they are (Proverbs 23:7). Countless others have uttered the same golden truth in different ways. I heard noted author Wayne Dyer say once, "Contemplate the conditions you wish to create in your life." Reverend Barbara King, founder and pastor of Hillside Chapel in Atlanta, Georgia, says, "You do get what you see, so you might as well see what you get." Benjamin Disraeli says, "Nurture your mind with great thoughts, for you will never go any higher than you think."

Spiritual and mental renewal are necessary in our demanding world. It is so easy to be bowled over by the endless challenges and expectations of everyday life. Many persons have responded to the accelerated pace and heavier load of life either by hurrying to keep up or by becoming numb to it all. Hurriedness and numbness are not our only options. There is a way to faithfully bring an alert, energized, and focused self to each new day.

This book is about our mindful and soulful second awakening. I have found a way to wake up the second time that has changed my life dramatically. This book is my attempt to share the gift of this life-changing spiritual discipline.

The Second Awakening

In his brilliant book, *Crossing the Unknown Sea: Work As a Pilgrimage of Identity,* David Whyte offers his interpretation of "a good waking":

> A good waking is a waking full of hearing, subtle song, and anticipation: the birdsong outside the house, the

luminous tone of the first spring light through the shut-
ters, or the sight of your partner's face familiar and slowly
coming to life again.

We should apprentice ourselves to coming awake,
treat it as a form of mastery.

The threshold of waking, the entry to the day, is the
musician's foot lifted to begin the beat.[1]

I hear "I waked up!" in Whyte's discussion of waking
up. And it is clear to me that he is referring to the second
waking: our response to the gift and grace of another day's
journey. Beneath Whyte's words is the presumption that our
waking needs to work for us rather than against us, and that
our decision to simply notice more can make a new world
of an old world.

Learning that we all wake up twice was a revelation for
me; discovering that I had the God-given power to determine
how I woke up the second time was liberation! Moreover, I
found that I had the power to make this second awakening,
to use Whyte's marvelous phrase, "a good waking."

Inspired by this new truth and freedom, I initially began
paying closer attention to my first thoughts and feelings. My
goal was to deflate negative mental and emotional reality
and inflate positive mental and emotional reality. I wanted
to breathe (a word which means "spirit") in and out the life
blessings I aspired to. Secondly, I initiated a daily morning
devotional discipline, involving prayer, scripture and other
inspirational reading, and journaling. Other elements were
added in time, including lighting a small candle, viewing
art, reading and writing poetry, and listening to music. My

morning devotional commenced at some point during my first hour of the day and took about fifteen to thirty minutes. There were days when I blew out the candle and noticed that an hour had gone by.

Leaning into my second awakening, learning about and cultivating it, transformed my life. I began feeling empowered in new and freeing ways. I did not have to be a branch blown this way and that way by the stressful winds of life. I had the power to fill my mind and heart with enlivening thoughts at daybreak. The initial filling, I discovered, had sticking power. The peace and energy established in the early morning hours were portable, facilitating peaceful inspirations at various intervals throughout the day.

I began experiencing astounding new spiritual and physical energy. I felt more peace and joy, more often. I began to see things more clearly, and became more in touch with a deepening understanding about myself and the world. Even on days when I was feeling less than buoyant, I felt more keenly and regularly aware of my life and my surroundings.

I felt more in control of my responses to life, especially my reactions to challenging people and situations. I connected this enhanced power over emotional reactions with the new practice of registering and regulating morning thoughts. I was beginning to use mental muscles I had never used before, resulting in enhanced mental strength throughout all areas of my life.

I began to feel more vividly God's love, self-love, and love for others. I began crying during some of my morning devotionals, not because I was sad, but because I was filled to running over with feelings of fresh acceptance and affection. Finally, I became more expressive, creative, and productive in my labor and leisure. Over a span of six years, I wrote five books and several other inspirational, educational resources. I created several new classes and workshops. In addition to expanding my leisure staples, reading books, and listening to music, I embarked on new journeys, including undertaking a study of jazz and poetry. Life became less like a recurring episode of the non-threatening and familiar and more like a rendezvous with the new and different. Life became an adventure. Reflecting back on that time, a promise Jesus once made to a woman at a well comes to mind: "but those who drink of the water that I will give them will never be thirsty. The water that I will give will become in them a spring of water gushing up to eternal life" (John 4:14).

My Morning Brew

It was during these morning devotions that I discovered the most soulfully filling and energizing drink I had ever tasted. I began referring to it as my morning brew. This time of thinking and feeling transformed my thoughts and feelings—the mental and emotional energies that in the end, as permitted by God, create the life I live. Perhaps this is the ultimate power of brew: it offers a simple method for regularly tapping into your spirit and allowing God's Spirit to influence your thoughts and feelings in transformative ways. Isn't this what Jesus did? He found ways into people, into their desires, intents, fears, longings, and hopes. He invited them to imagine things they had never dreamed of. His deep impact on the souls of people was so thoroughly freeing and enlivening that his resurrection, unbeknown to his killers, was a given. God and creative life will not be stopped.

As I continued to practice drinking my morning brew, I learned that I could mix the brew and drink it each day, experiencing a different taste and touch of potent loving renewal from head to toe. I noticed that the drink's potency was not in proportion to the amount of time I spent drinking it. There were mornings when five to ten minutes of brew seemed to excavate and activate a hidden source of strength inside me. Other mornings allowed for longer and thus deeper searches into the depths of my feelings, questions, and longings. Usually my brew lasted about twenty minutes, and usually there was something soulfully attractive about it that kept me coming back for more.

Finally, I discovered that though I had a full cup of brew in the morning, I could take sips of it throughout the day. At work, I could focus on creating and experiencing a restorative moment of soulful respite. While living my day, I could reflect on and experience God's love through noticing nature or the baby smiling at me in the airport. At all points throughout the day, I discovered I could take a moment to thank God for the person I was and the person I was becoming. I could take a moment to nod to the person passing by me in a show of human affirmation and even bow toward them in my spirit. I found that as I welcomed the morning, I could also welcome any moment that I pleased and whatever it held.

I discovered that even the mourning moments are to be savored. Sadness is a part of life that must be noticed in order to learn the things we can learn only in the places of brokenness. So while brew was at first a morning blessing, I soon discovered that it was a lasting, lingering, and loitering blessing.

Brew became the process B.R.E.W.: *B*eing still, *R*eceiving God's love, *E*mbracing my personhood, and *W*elcoming the day. B.R.E.W. is a divine power drink for your soul, and your innermost thoughts and feelings. Let B.R.E.W. fill your soul!

2. MORNING B.R.E.W.:

The Power Drink
You Can't Buy in a Store

"But those who wait for the Lord shall renew their strength, they shall mount up with wings like eagles, they shall run and not be weary, they shall walk and not faint."
—Isaiah 40:31

"The Bird's wings are undoubtedly very well designed indeed, but it is . . . the marvelous skill with which they are used. The soaring problem is apparently not so much one of better wings as of better operators."
—Wilbur Wright

"There's a feeling here inside that I cannot hide and I know I've tried, but it's turning me around. . . . I am gonna be alright as soon as I get home."
—Charlie Smalls, *Soon As I Get Home*

The Discovery

As I became more committed to my new morning waking up discipline, I began to chart my most noteworthy experiences.

Noteworthy did not always mean an experience that left me feeling like I could leap tall buildings in a single bound. It did not always mean breakthrough enlightenment and enthusiastic merry-making in the morning. With all due respect to blaring trumpets and bright lights, the truly wonderful can be slight, gentle, and barely noticeable. The greatest unheralded gift of all is a gentle touch. Whether ebullient or ever so soft in its manifestation, I discovered a pattern forming in my brief morning rituals. Four elements seemed to present themselves as fundamental to my process: *B*eing still, *R*eceiving God's love, *E*mbracing my personhood, and, in the spirit of Jared's proclamation "I waked up!", *W*elcoming the day. This is where the acronym B.R.E.W. comes from.

I began building my devotional experience around these four elements, making sure that I spent a few minutes each morning focused on each one. I discovered that just a few minutes of mental solitude cultivated a peace and creative power that I had not known before. Morning B.R.E.W. proceeded to transform my life. It continues to do so each day.

Being Still

Let me introduce you to the elements, the ingredients, of Morning B.R.E.W. First, there is **being still**. Being still is the bedrock of B.R.E.W. It is the taste that initiates and enriches the other tastes. Being still is more than being physically motionless; it is about establishing a sense of mental motionlessness. As I was beginning to practice Morning B.R.E.W., I realized that my morning time was the most peaceful time of the day. It was a homecoming of sorts. Images of me as a child enjoying solitude under a tree in my backyard returned to me. I saw myself lying on a park green in Amarillo, Texas, having stolen away from our high school choir to just be. Stillness felt like home. It was a home that offered several connected, enchanting rooms, namely awareness, clarity, enlightenment, and divine affirmation.

Just this morning, I experienced being still in a way that so inspired me that I must tell you about it. I awakened with a start, in part, prompted by a disturbing dream. As I moved to the back porch, I began my morning ritual of first establishing mental and emotional stillness. As I sat there, elements of the dream surfaced, followed by a line of living issues related to familial changes and transitions. In the stillness, I mentally counted the number of matters vying for my attention. Each matter was beginning to conjure worry and anxiety inside me. Noting my mounting tension, I simply held it all for a moment, just as it was. And in the stillness, two decibels above a whisper, I heard this: "Look for adventure in adversity." Immediately, I felt a definite lightening of heart and spirit.

I proceeded to accept this surprise invitation by beginning to imagine at least one lesson to be learned in each of the matters before me. Before long the mysterious encouragement to look for adventure in adversity had become a living reality, formidable enough to lift me out of the dump I was descending into. In the stillness, transformation filled my being from head to toe; I was energized. There was something else. I will not shy away from telling you that at the end of it all, in my spirit I felt an angelic being smiling, winking, and turning away toward eternity. This is what happened to me just this morning. And this is why I want you to learn to practice stillness with sacred purposefulness and intentionality. Stillness is our greatest hidden strength.

Receiving God's Love

Early Morning Mist
Early morning mist
barely noticeable.

Stop wincing to see,
walk out into God's gentle rain.
—K.B.J.

The second element of B.R.E.W. is **receiving God' love.** This second ingredient is what I believe the sacred wink was all about. (You will find out soon enough that the B.R.E.W. elements intermix with each other.) In my imagination, when the heavenly being winked and smiled it facilitated my latest experience of God's great love for me. My eyes are moistening as I write this because experiencing unconditional love every day revives every day. It is one thing to sing, "Jesus loves me this I know, for the Bible tells me so." It is something else alltogether wonderful to experience that love each day, at the start of the day.

I used to think that as a husband, father, and clergyman, my first, middle, and last actions of the day were to be in service to others. Living my life that way for years culminated in great service, but great service is not our only calling in life. Moreover, contrary to what you might believe, it is not the first calling. The first calling in life is not to give anyone anything; the first calling in life is to receive God's glorious acceptance and affection. When this truth came home to me, I was home in a new and deeply fulfilling way. So each morning's B.R.E.W. experience includes moments of relishing God's love through mental reflection and visualization.

Through the years, I have imagined receiving God's love in many different ways, including backstroking in God's loving waters or standing under a waterfall of God's grace, even imagining God kissing me gently on my head and saying what jazz great, Duke Ellington, used to say to the audience at the conclusion of each performance, "We love you madly."

In the forthcoming chapter on receiving God's love, you will learn how to create your own sacred love images. You will learn how to disperse them in your life and lean into them with all of your heart. You will come to know the power of such sacred love images for creating esteem, kindness, work, joy, and leisure gladness. You will come to know, if you don't already, that the biblical legend David does not have a monopoly on Psalm 23:5: "My cup overflows."

What Difference Would It Make?

What if in God's bosom, there is an ocean full of love?
What if you could drink from that ocean each day,
as much as you wanted,
anytime that you wanted,
for as often as you wanted?
What difference would it make?
—K.B.J.

Embracing Your Personhood

As I write this, three of our magnificent offspring, Jared, Joya, and Jovonna, are online reviewing a list of top colleges. They are excited to find several of their choice schools in the top rankings. How do you rank yourself? How high is your self-esteem? On our kitchen bulletin board there is a family calendar sent to us at the beginning of the year by my brother and sister-in-law, Gerald and Elizabeth Brown. Each month features a thematic picture. The picture for August is of a palm with a big heart in the middle of it. What do you see when you look at the palms of your hands? What do you feel?

B.R.E.W. is about enhancing awareness through being still, receiving divine acceptance, and **embracing your personhood.** This third ingredient of B.R.E.W. is a natural result of drinking in the prior two ingredients. It's hard to embrace fresh truth and a fresh experience with God without spilling grace all over yourself. The grace that you feel flowing over you is God's grace and your own as you truly embrace your personhood. Learning to grace ourselves is a necessary action. As I have contended in two prior books, *Rest in the Storm: Self-Care Strategies for Clergy and Other Caregivers* and *Addicted to Hurry: Spiritual Strategies for Slowing Down*, such self-focus is not about selfishness but *sacred self-is-ness.*

Computer gaming is something I do for the fun of it. Sports games are my favorite. My second favorite games are role playing/adventure games. In many of these games it is essential for your character to be outfitted in protective gear and carry weapons and health potions substantive enough to face new, often dangerous challenges. Being insufficiently equipped guarantees a swift "Game Ended" screen.

Embracing your personhood each day is a way of dressing your soul and equipping your spirit. It involves remembering who you are and affirming your *essential self* as well as your *emerging self.* It invites you to be honest about your weaknesses and no less honest about your strengths. Embracing your personhood dares you to see yourself as strong and becoming stronger in God's love.

Embracing who *you* are is just one side of the B.R.E.W. personhood experience. Embracing others, including those you may be having problems with, is the other side. The experience of embracing others can free you in amazing, life-giving ways. For example, several weeks ago I did a workshop in North Carolina. During the presentations, one person seemed irritated by it all. He asked me a single question that indicated a basic rejection of my thoughts and a critical regard toward my points. An attempt to greet him in the hall between classes was met with a curt response. Though the workshop was a huge success overall, the image and feeling of this man's sharp edge remained with me. It wasn't just that he seemed to disagree with me, I also sensed that he disliked like me. Even though I have learned that needing people to like you is a huge stumbling block, I still feel a sting when I feel rejected.

A few days later while I was embracing personhood, my own and others, I saw this person in my mind and, like before, he was not smiling. Nonetheless, I did what the B.R.E.W. moment was encouraging me to do: I embraced him in my spirit. I don't know if he smiled; I know that I did. I know that in that moment the toxic poison of bitterness was rendered impotent inside me.

Even if we can't embrace persons physically, we can always embrace them emotionally and spiritually. It is one of the healthiest and holiest things we can do for others and ourselves. Martin Luther King Jr. said once:

> We are all tied together in a single garment of destiny. I
> can't be who I ought to be until you are who you ought
> to be. And, you can't be who you ought to be until I am
> who I ought to be.[2]

The third motion of B.R.E.W., embracing personhood, is a way of clasping and adorning yourself with the sacred garments of personhood and community each day. It is about meeting God daily to love yourself toward your best self.

Welcoming the Day

The final ingredient of B.R.E.W. is the element that started it all. Jared's morning acclamation was a way of **welcoming the arrival of another day.** In the final motion of B.R.E.W. you welcome not just some days, but each day. Think about it. As a culture we have given some days favored day status. Holidays and Fridays are usually in this group. But other days are not just diminished, they are essentially damned. We refer to the first work day of the week as "Blue Monday." Wednesday has been called "Hump Day," because it is in the middle of the week. That's 104 days out of 365 days that we virtually write off. Add to that number days we unconsciously, if not consciously, look over in anticipation of big celebration days, days that we would shove aside if we could to get to the day we can't wait for. When it's all counted up, we miss a sizable potion of our daily life as we lunge for the future.

One way to insure that we are alive to each new day is to pay attention to each new day "from the get go." One of the staples in my African American church worship tradition is something called the welcome address. This is a brief statement of greeting given to persons who are visiting the church for the first time. The welcomes can be as simple as the legendary sonnet typically performed by children:

You're welcome once.
You're welcome twice.
You're welcome three times in the name of Jesus Christ.
You're welcome, welcome, welcome.

My favorite welcome addresses were more elaborate, almost mini-sermons. After these were delivered, you knew you were welcome. Even the members who came to church every Sunday felt a new embracing. The persons who gave these kinds of welcome addresses leaned into every word and punctuated their saying with spirit and smiles. After a welcome like this, the whole church usually erupted in resounding "Amens" and sometimes applause.

Welcoming the day has become intensely important to me. I find that entering the day with positive and generous feelings has a significant impact on the quality of my day. Early welcoming can set a positive, powerful tone that can flavor the entire day. This places a new creative spin on life. Life is not just what happens; life is what we call into existence, beginning with our first feelings for the morning. Become an observer of this. Begin to chronicle your initial thoughts and feelings as you wake up. Pay attention to how what you think and feel informs the morning you actually have. Welcoming can be the difference between abundant living and so-so existence.

The welcome address is the first part of a two-part piece. In many churches, a designated visitor has prepared a response to the welcome. My favorite responders always started speaking before they arrived at the microphone. Rising from their pew, they would begin quoting Scripture while walking, "I was glad when they said to me, 'Let us go to the house of the Lord!'" (Psalm 122:1). In the black church, if someone starts talking before they reach the microphone, look out! You are in for a few minutes (sometimes longer) of inspiring spirited oratory. Each new day deserves a welcome address. And if we are sincere, we will receive a response, a morning refreshing, soothing, and enlivening to the soul.

A Daily Spiritual Adventure

Who was it that said, "Predictability and familiarity are two unsung sins"? I just did. And I mean it tenaciously. Nowhere is same-ness more prevalent than in the area of our religious devotional practice. Why does spiritual practice have to be burdensome and, even worse, boring? And, by the way, I have discovered that neither complexity nor simplicity has a monopoly on religious boredom. We can be stuck in seminaries in the metropolis and churches by the roadside. In churches, seminaries, and homes, we can easily repeat the same words, prayers, songs, and sentiments without ever becoming sickened by our passivity. We repeat these things out of a sense of homage and the need to tether ourselves to things that we know (tradition) lest we be blown away by the winds of change and difference. Feeding this unconsciously feared malady is driven by something submerged even deeper in our unconscious, the need to hold onto control by any means necessary, including keeping newness at arm's length.

Sameness must be denied! Life at its best is about forsaking the known for the unknown. At its finest and fullest, life is about flinging ourselves into experiences, ideas, and places we may have never even heard of before. How virtuous is sameness in an ever-changing world spun by an incessantly creative God? As a spark from the candle leaps toward the place where I am writing, I am reminded of the closing declaration I make on my Web site, www.playandsoar.com: I would rather live one day on fire than a lifetime bored to death.

B.R.E.W. has been the most adventurous spiritual practice I have ever experienced. Even though it consists of just four basic elements, the lengths, experiences, and variations of those elements are endless. I have often been energized from head to toe by just a couple of minutes with a single element. It has challenged me to dig my own inner wells of refreshment and imagination. It has prodded me to understand independence and interdependence in deeply spiritual ways. B.R.E.W. has been and continues to be a boundary buster for me on every front of my life. I have fallen in love with the sight of drifting limits.

B.R.E.W. is probably different from any other morning devotional book that you have read. Get ready for the new adventure! I challenge you, through God's grace, to take responsibility for creating new spiritual adventures. While I have benefited and continue to be strengthened by standard devotional texts, most of them share an unintended weakness: they promote "devotional watching." If we are not careful, our devotions can become a time of passively observing the ideas and words of others. Even our culminating prayer is often borrowed from the faith experience of others.

Devotional books are best used when they inspire us to cultivate our own personal experience with God and life. B.R.E.W. is distinctive because of its creative capacity and impulse. It is not a passive experience involving reading and reflecting on the views of others. You create your B.R.E.W., new insightful impressions of God and life, with your head and heart each time you drink it. You are not sipping the work of others; you are drinking from your own inner wells of sacred refreshment and imagination. These are wells you dig day in and day out. Thus, you will get out of B.R.E.W. what God will grace you and what you imagine, think, and will into it.

When you think of *Morning B.R.E.W.,* I don't want you to think first of a book authored by Kirk Byron Jones. I want you to think of your own daily deepening, energizing, and transformative experience. In this sense—and I believe this with all my heart—B.R.E.W. is less my book; B.R.E.W. is more your experience.

B.R.E.W. Is Your Experience

B.R.E.W. will be as meaningful, diverse, and spiritually transforming as you imagine and allow it to be. Inspired by God's love and your longing, B.R.E.W. will be your breakthrough creation for each new day. I will share some of my experiences, some of them deeply personal, but your work with B.R.E.W. and its work with you will be uniquely different from my own. Glory hallelujah for that! How could it be the same, given our uniquely sacred internal components and wirings, and given the different challenges that we face in our lives?

Some practices of B.R.E.W. are more predominant than others in my experience. For example, I have come to rely heavily on creative visualizations in each of B.R.E.W.'s essential elements. Likewise, poetry has become a frequent outflow of my B.R.E.W. time. For this reason I could not envision producing this manuscript without poetry. Other practices may shine brighter for you. Pay attention and drink with great freedom and joy from those wells that inspire you most.

Finally, before you disembark onto the mainland of the text, I pray that this new spiritual discipline will become for you what it has become for me, a form of spiritual adventuring. I believe we have come to this world for adventures, for the arrival or advent of new occurrences, and for the invigorating, if threatening, risks of new discoveries. I discovered soon after starting my B.R.E.W. ritual that it held the mysterious power to take me somewhere exotic and different each time I practiced it. B.R.E.W. has remained with me and I with it because each experience with it is unique, sometimes dramatically so.

Each experience with B.R.E.W. affords me the prospect of new sightings of mystery, God, myself, others, and our world. Some mornings, I am filled by familiar images that feed me in fresh new ways. Other mornings, startling new visualizations, feelings, and impressions make my old world a new world. If you think all of this is serious and heavy, think again. Some of my best experiences with B.R.E.W. have had me laughing within, if not aloud.

In fact, I laughed this morning. As I was visualizing God's love, a scene from a few days ago replayed itself in my mind. My family and I were riding to Cape Cod, Massachusetts, when we noticed a plane carrying a banner. The banner was large, seemingly longer and wider than the plane that was bearing it along. The marketing message for a cable network company was boldly clear. Well, that plane flew again this morning in my mental sky. This time with a different pilot (God) and a different message ("I LOVE YOU").

What difference does God's love make? The difference is in the acceptance; the difference is in the healing; the difference is in the power. This difference has extraordinary social as well as personal benefits. Feeling accepted creates a welcoming spirit inside of me. Having been healed, I can and want to extend healing to others. Having been spiritually energized and filled with the marvelously concentrated energy that created the cosmos, I can face it all with an ever increasing fearlessness and with the courage to create. Like Jeremiah, the prophet of old, I feel like there's "something like a burning fire shut up in my bones" (Jeremiah 20:9).

3. Being Still:

The Power in the Pause

"Be still, and know that I am God!"
—Psalm 46:10

"Those of steadfast mind you keep in peace—in peace because they trust in you."
—Isaiah 26:3

"I know the soft wind will blow me home."
—Yu Hsuan-chi

"How good it is to center down! To sit quietly and see one's self pass by!"
—Howard Thurman

"It's not what you say, it's what goes on between the lines."
—Dame Judith Dench, Oscar winning actress

An Exercise in Stillness

I have an exercise for you. Remember B.R.E.W. is not a book, it is an experience. The following page is yours to create. Here are the directions. Feel free to modify them in ways that will enhance your experience:

1. Write the words "silence" and "stillness" in the center of the page. As an alternative, you may wish to sketch or doodle images of these realities. Whether writing or drawing, don't limit yourself to a regular pencil or pen. Use crayons or other instruments that bring color and creativity to the exercise.

2. Write and/or draw any thought, idea, or image that your center depiction of silence/stillness inspires. Use as much time as you desire. B.R.E.W. and hurry don't mix.

Ideas and Images

Reflecting on Your Experience

Take some moments to reflect on your ideas and/or images.

What were the first things you placed on the page?

Are your images of silence and stillness more positive or negative?

Can you think of something to add or take away?

What surprises you and why?

You may be surprised by a number of negative images you have written down regarding silence. I will never forget a moment during a class I taught on the great theologian and preacher, Howard Thurman, in which a student reminded us that silence may be a threat to some because of prior linkages of silence and negative experiences. For many, silence represents the calm before the storm of another violent encounter with an abusive parent or spouse. In our culture, silence is associated with mental diminishment, non-productivity, and suspicious behavior. For some, coming home to the wellspring of sacred silence will mean crossing over significant obstructions.

Sharing My Experience

I did this word exercise just before beginning to write this chapter. This is what my word arrangement looked like:

Negative/   Inspiration
Positive
Connotations

                            Contentment

                Limpness
                Comfort
        Candle

SILENCE/STILLNESS
                        Hushing
                        Stone
Reception

    Clarity   Breath
                    Breathing
                    Vulnerability

                    Humility
Emptying
        Rest   Grace

Release   Restoration

Let me tell you about a few of these words and what they mean to my B.R.E.W. experience.

Limpness

I cannot get away from this term when describing the essence of my experience of being still. I find a comfortable place and consciously relax my muscles. I begin to breathe more deliberately, noticing each breath I take. I let the breaths take me. I release control of my body to the comfort of the moment. My experience is akin to a team-building exercise in which you daringly fall back into the waiting arms of a co-worker. You can fall back as a stiff hard board, or you can fall back easy, like a leaf dropping effortlessly from a tree. Howard Thurman once prayed:

> As the sea gull lays in the wind current,
> so I lay myself into the spirit of God.[3]

Limpness, a loosening of anxiety and tension, soul and mental freedom, is what I have come to own as my *home feeling* during morning times of stillness and silence.

I have since learned that a state of limpness is an entryway to a mental state that is greatly supportive of clarity and creative breakthroughs. Scientists have identified four basic brain wave states: beta, alpha, theta, and delta. Beta waves are associated with our natural everyday waking state of mind. Our minds produce alpha waves when we are relaxed. You are in an alpha state when you are daydreaming and generally taking it easy. The brain moves into a third state, a theta brain wave state, when we are experiencing dreaming sleep or deep meditation. Delta waves are what we give off when we are at our deepest level of sleep.

The last two brain wave states, theta and delta, are facilitated through sleep and through intentionally willing our conscious minds to be at ease. Easing our conscious minds loosens our unconscious and supra-conscious minds, our deeper sources of unlimited and sometimes uncanny wisdom and knowledge. This explains why some of our best ideas and solutions to problems arrive when we are not thinking about it, and why hashing something around again and again in our minds sometimes seems to make matters worse. This is not an argument against rational thought, but for thought that transcends rationality. I believe this is in part because of what Albert Einstein is reported to have said, "Imagination is more important than knowledge." We are our thoughts, but not *just our thoughts.*

B.R.E.W. limpness helps us to access our God-given "theta-ness" and "delta-ness," enabling us to tap into the kind of power and energy that Jesus talked about in ways that puzzled and inspired: "It is your Father's good pleasure to give you the kingdom" (Luke 12:32). "The water that I will give will become in them a spring of water gushing up to eternal life" (John 4:14). "[You] will do greater works" (John 14:12)

Notice the intensity of the blessings. Not just pleasure, but "good pleasure." Not just water, but "gushing water." Not just life, but "eternal life." Not just works, "but greater works." Reflecting on this helps us to comprehend and receive God's bountiful blessings. Such bounty cannot be received by souls that are hardened, rigid, and tight. We must loosen up emotionally, mentally, and spiritually to live. Limpness loosens us. Imagine the morning B.R.E.W. limpness loosening you up for new life.

How limp should you be? Once during a workshop, I was talking about resting in God when an elderly gentlemen asked if he could come forward. He then asked that a chair be placed in the center of the room. As he sat down in the chair, we all observed him with great curiosity. He proceeded to tell a story about the legendary boxing manager, Angelo Dundee, famed corner man for Muhammad Ali and many others. Once, as Dundee was riding in a rural area, he noticed a woman in a rocking chair on a porch. She appeared motionless, so motionless that Dundee felt like she may have expired. He asked the driver to stop the car, and he approached where the woman was seated. As he came closer, he realized, with no small relief that she was breathing. In that moment, she stirred. Assuring her that he meant her no harm, Dundee explained to the elderly woman that he thought something was wrong with her because of the way she was sleeping. The woman smiled and said, "Well, when I works, I works hard, and when I rest, I rest loose." How limp should you be? As loose as you can possibly be. As loose as an old lady sleeping loose and easy in a rocking chair.

Emptying

Do something for me. Think of someone you love. Now, image them in your mind. Next, think of one of your favorite places in the entire world. Now, image that place in your mind, drawing as minimal or detailed a picture as you desire. You have just exercised one of your greatest powers: the ability to create mental images of envisioned reality. Your loved one did not have to be present for you to see him or her. You did not have to be in your favorite room or even near it to effectively create it in your own mind.

This power to mentally create whatever we desire is nothing less than extraordinary. The problem is we tend to use it negatively or not at all. We use it negatively when we imagine the worst. We can create some of the worst case scenarios in the world in our minds. In so doing, we become chronic victims of things that never happen, or worse, victims of negative fortune that we abet through woeful mental envisioning. The late great comedian, Flip Wilson, used to say, "What you see is what you get." In her popular work, *Creative Visualization,* Shakti Gawain writes, "We always attract in our lives whatever we think about the most, believe in most strongly, expect on the deepest levels, and/or imagine most vividly."[4] Proverbs 23:7 puts it this way, "For as he thinks in his heart, so *is* he."

Just as mental imaging or visualization may be used negatively, it can be used in more helpful, even astounding ways. Chinese pianist Liu Chi Kung was imprisoned and banned from playing the piano for seven years during the Cultural Revolution. Upon his release, persons were amazed at Kung's seemingly undiminished musical prowess. Asked how it was possible to maintain his musical mastery when he was denied access to playing for so long, Kung responded, "I did practice every day. I rehearsed every piece I had ever played, note by note, in my mind."[5]

In Matthew 22:37, Jesus locates the essence of religious law in loving God with soul, heart, and mind. B.R.E.W. allows you to mindfully manifest and grow your faith through mental visualization. Mental visualization is one of the primary instruments in your B.R.E.W.

tool box. In my experience, it's not how detailed or how long the visualization is, but rather how real it is. If your visualization can absorb you for just a few moments, you will have accessed an extraordinary power for living. Just as with anything else, the more you practice visualization the better you will become at it. I interpret better to mean an increasing ability to create varied sorts of mental pictures and a greater talent for putting images on your mental screen with ease.

You will discover ways to use mental imaging during all four phases of B.R.E.W., beginning with the first phase, being still. What you want to visualize during B.R.E.W. stillness is emptiness. Here is an exercise that may help get you started. On a blank sheet of paper, take a moment to make a list of everything that emptiness conjures up in your mind. When you are done, glean ten images of emptiness from your list and write them on the lines provided.

_____   _____

_____   _____

_____   _____

_____   _____

_____   _____

Why do I want you to have images of emptiness at your disposal? Emptiness makes for a great beginning. I want you to experience palpable freedom from everything for a few moments each morning. As best as you can, you must let go of everything, all of your thoughts and feelings. It is vital that you do not begin your days feeling overwhelmed. You must start each day feeling just the opposite: at ease with yourself and the world. In a world of chronic overload and hurry, stillness is a mighty asset that facilitates emptiness of mind and heart. Emptying allows you to begin each day of your life from a place of peace.

Emptying also allows for cleansing. One of my images of emptying is of a swamp being drained. I am from the swampland of Louisiana and, for me, emptiness is a time of draining worries, fears, and narrow and negative thinking away from my being. Sometimes I envision emptiness as a clear sky. With this image in mind, I am brought to a place of renewed mental clarity and focus. One of my favorite images of emptiness is an unfurnished house. This image brings home to me the need to un-clutter, un-load, and un-stuff my life. It helps me to enter the day with a certain spiritual lightness of heart. You will have your favorite images of emptiness. Feed them and let them feed you.

Before leaving this section on emptying, there is something else you must know. I once had a dream in which our third daughter, Joya, fell from a bridge into some shallow water. Without thinking, I jumped into the water and "saved" her. I woke up dutifully proud that I had performed my instinctive and natural parental function. But then, as I lay in the bed, something hit me from within, "You prevented her from learning how to swim." The dream took on more meaning as I realized how it related to my current relationship with Joya. We were preparing to send her to France for an academic year. My parental role was changing. The dream was, in fact, asking me to empty myself of my protective parental role in order to grasp a new role as a spiritually supportive father from afar. I was jarred to new truth and life.

This dream comes to mind as I tell you this: *You must be prepared to empty yourself of previous, familiar images of God, to embrace new, unfamiliar images of God.* Whatever you know of God is *not* God. God is always more and beyond. We stifle our devotional lives when we allow them to be governed by fixed and entrenched images of God. Besides being Ultimate Reality, "God" is our perception of ultimate reality. Closed images of "God," no matter how comforting and majestic, are still closed, restricting, and, ultimately, living-limited. For at least a brief moment in time every day, we need an experience of God untainted by our narrow prejudices and beliefs. We need to let God be God on God's terms. Those terms are always, in the words of the folk theology I heard in the church of my youth, Mount Hermon Baptist Church of New Orleans, Louisiana:

So high you can't get over them
So wide, you can't go around them, and
So low, you can't go under them.

How else can we grow in our knowledge of God unless there is always more to know about God? If we are ever able to "arrive" concerning God, how mysterious and tremendous was that God to begin with?

Emptying is a time of purposefully not knowing all that we know about God, in order to know again, for the first time. Be still, become empty, and know that God is God. The poet Gillian Conoley once said, "I find myself very attracted to poetry that has a lot of white space lately, I find that sort of work restful. Not to have a page covered with words is somehow more inviting; I want to go into that world." Conoley then asked a halting question: "What if there is not enough nothing?"[6]

Where there is not enough nothing, our "somethings" rule the day as undisputed truth. Their reign could not be further from the truth, especially where God is concerned. The B.R.E.W. empty spaces we experience are about our making room for the more that is always, always there, the more beyond words that carries us from where we are to where we aspire and long to be. Your emptiness determines your openness.

Closed spirituality is breathless spirituality. Religion cluttered by excessive, often oppressive and dehumanizing rhetoric, is choking. More than any other time in world history, religion and spirituality need to breathe in new air, fresh winds of grace and acceptance, or we will die having suffocated from poisoned, prejudiced notions of divinity and divine will.

At first you may find this God emptiness unnerving and, perhaps, even unfaithful. Yet in time you will (I hope) learn to acquire its new tastes as an essential part of your spiritual growth. Growth is the central word. As long as the term "God" conjures the exact same images in your mind, you risk limiting yourself to the exact same experiences resulting in no real spiritual growth. On the other hand, empty your mind of all that you know for just a few moments and you open yourself up to all there is, including that which lies beyond your normal everyday experience with God.

Where God is concerned, we always ought to be hearing new notes, pauses, and dissonances even, sounds that upon first hearing appear discordant and strange. For example, most of us have some image of God as a comforter. What would it mean for you to have alternative images of God as something other than a comforter? What about God as a beggar outside a bus station? What about God as a joker, finding fanciful ways to jar us out of our sacred stupors of conformity. Threatening? Absolutely. Better than stale sameness? You bet.

By intentionally, if momentarily, emptying ourselves of what we know all too well about God, we experience God in deeper, wider ways. Emptiness deepens and widens us for new beats, sounds, and rhythms about God. Our known sacred music is just that—our known sacred music. Explosive spiritual renewal lies beyond the small valley of what we know, toward the vast uncharted land of the unknown. Beyond the boundaries are the places that are awaiting your daring, if trepid, journeying each new day.

Vulnerability and Openness

A third word I wrote when I did the silence/stillness exercise is the word "vulnerability." Upon rereading that word I had to think about what I really meant. If I did the exercise again I would place another word beside it. What I mean by vulnerability is openness. I was listening to a gospel album the other day and was surprised by a request made by the singer to the audience. He invited persons to "open up their spirits" to the musical experience. Stillness opens the spirit for the grace of holy reverie and the gift of divine company.

During B.R.E.W. stillness time, watch and feel as limpness flows into emptiness, and emptiness into openness. Limpness is your relaxed soul, emptiness is your cleansed soul, and openness is your welcoming soul. When you pass a store and there's a sign out that reads "open," that's not just a designation verifying current status; it is an invitation to come in and shop. Openness is a welcome sign to Loving Mystery, an invitation to come in, sit awhile and have their way with us. This is a necessary, prerequisite to vulnerability; there is no discovery, learning, and growth without openness.

If we are to be open in life for growth, we must make ourselves open. Why? The default position for most of us is "closed." I don't believe we start out that way. I want to believe that when we are born we are set on "open." The proof is the innate curiosity and "why-ness" of most toddlers. But then something happens. We go to school. We learn conformity. We learn rote memorization. We learn how to merely make and meet the grade. The unintended result of "education" for many is a dissolving of an early drive to dig and discover. We become passive repositories of information instead of active explorers of the unknown and beyond. Instead of connecting old knowledge to create new knowledge, we settle for regurgitating the things we know and resisting things that may challenge our comfortableness. We become people of the rut.

Resetting your internal learning switch to "open" is the best way to get out of a rut. B.R.E.W. offers you a chance to do this each day. Each day, as part of your stillness, you may reaffirm a posture of openness to the world. You may do this by leaning into your emptiness; notice it, feel it, savor it. When the void inside you is at its finest and fullest, proclaim that empty, vacant space as open to the fresh winds of the Spirit.

I have been stretched and strengthened by other people's insights into openness. Tilden Edwards writes about the need to live with "open hope":

> We never know just what the loving truth is until it is shown us as we go through the day from situation to situation. Therefore, our hope is not focused on particular expectations or results; it is more open and available to what we do not know and do not need to know until the time comes. . . . Such wide-eyed, open hope frees us to be more in touch with what is of God during the day, rather than being in touch with what we have predetermined by our too controlling and narrow expectations.[7]

The musings of jazz artists have been a deep and refreshing well for me on the value of openness. You may read more about this in my book, *The Jazz of Preaching: How to Preach with Great Freedom and Joy.* Here is a recent sentiment from that sacred circus of openness popularly known as jazz. Notice the connection bassist Miroslav Vitous makes between silence and freedom while discussing his new attitude about the play of not playing the bass:

This is where the bass doesn't play all the time. It's again breaking the traditional role of the bass, basically to set everybody free. When the bass stops playing, all of a sudden everybody's much more free because you have an equal thing going among the great musicians, and there's no one playing roles anymore. Immediately the drums become more free. Everybody becomes more free. It's a very liberating process.[8]

We are so used to connecting productivity with unceasing effort. How compelling and refreshing to have not just mere productivity, but majestic new creativity linked to the work of worklessness.

Awareness: A Hidden Benefit

Most lists are incomplete. Perhaps you noticed that the last time you returned home from a trip to the grocery store. When I reviewed my list of words related to silence and stillness, I sensed that something significant was missing. That something is best captured by the word "awareness." Though absent from my initial inventory, awareness is a mighty, but perhaps hidden, benefit of morning solitude. Even when I have not reached deep or high levels of limpness, emptiness, and openness, being still always stirs in me a deeper awareness of who I am and where I am.

Awareness tells me that I am, and that I am a particular person, in a particular place, at a particular time. How important is this? Have you ever seen a boxer attempting to get up after being knocked down? He or she has ten seconds to come to themselves, to regain a verifiable clarity about their identity and surroundings. This basic living awareness must be persuasive enough to convince the referee or else the bout is over. The same is true for each of us.

Awareness, a fundamental knowledge that we are, who we are, and where we are, is basic to living consciously and responsibly. Knowing that, who, and where we are and assuming responsibility for this knowledge are the perquisites for *the choice:* the decision to live with enthusiasm, the choice to be spirited by love and joy every morning of every day. Living without awareness is tantamount to going through life as a dazed boxer, listless, lifeless, and unable to come to life because we are unable (sometimes unwilling) to come to ourselves.

Soft Vigilance

I came across this phase in the writings of Ellen Langer. A proponent of mindfulness, living purposefully aware, and welcoming of new information, Langer suggests that we do well to have a mindset that is not overly locked on anything, so that we are free to pick up the surprise unsuspecting thoughts that can occur anywhere at any time. I want to suggest a sort of soft vigilance for B.R.E.W. stillness time. Your primary intent is to be empty and open. In my experience, such openness beckons profound insight from God, from our intuitions, from the thoughts that are always in the air around us, and from mystery. Sometimes these thoughts have been so exciting, either for their insight or for their fulfillment of a pressing desire in me that I have not been able to resist attending to them by writing them down, by speaking them into a recorder, or by making a mental note to myself to recall them soon after my emptying time is over. What am I saying? Paradoxically, during your brief moment of not attending to anything at all, pay attention ever so softly and gently to what arises.

The Jolt of Stillness

If you are not used to stillness or struggle with solitude, moments of silence on a regular basis will challenge you. You may be tempted to give up on being still because of the discomfort. Attempt to persevere by riding through the place of initial dis-ease. Breakthrough growth often begins in the tension of the familiar rubbing up against the unfamiliar.

Being still for small periods of time and doing so regularly will serve you well. Initially, try holding mental stillness for a few minutes. Use a timer to help you. When the bell rings, stop. After a few weeks, begin to add more minutes to this period until you are up to at least five to seven minutes of as complete and thorough a mind and spiritual ease as you can get. Five to seven minutes of each phase of B.R.E.W. is manageable for most people and offers an optimum spiritual and emotional experience.

Observing mental stillness for a small period every day will cultivate your capacity for stillness as well as your thirst for it. The more you do it, the more skilled at it you will become. And the more you do it, the more you will taste its deliciously empowering fruit. The desire for the fruit of stillness will motivate you toward a deepening experience.

I am convinced that deep levels of soul connectedness are accessible to all, not just "the spiritually anointed and appointed." With all due respect to persons who feel called to spending hours honing and refining their spiritual toning and tuning, you don't have to be an accomplished practitioner of meditation and other religious skills to feel the sacred in a very real way.

One of the great contributions of Jesus was his "de-specializing" of religion. His everyday ministry to everyday people deeply disturbed professionally accomplished religionists, precisely because he proclaimed a way that was open to all and accessible by all, even religious outcasts. Jesus preached and practiced that spiritual prosperity was not bestowed based on rigorous accomplishment, but mere openness of heart. He preached and practiced a grace that was in all and for all. The valve for releasing grace was not arduous ritual but genuine desire and receptivity. Deep spiritual connectedness is not something available to a few especially disciplined and devoted adherents. We are all spiritual beings. Spiritual stillness is openness and patience. You don't need an extensive course or degree for this; you simply need belief and the simple holy deed of honest desire.

Practicing Silence: A Guided Exercise

I invite you to join me in a practice of silence. Find a comfortable place and assume a relaxed posture. Shake your arms out. Turn your neck from side to side. Firm and loosen various sections of your body. Take a few deep breaths. Let your body feel free from having to carry you, from having to support you.

After coming to a place of relative physical comfort, stop yourself from thinking about anything and everything for a few moments. You will create and discover your own best methods for doing this. For now, simply picture your mind as a VCR or DVD player. Your thoughts are moving through at your normal rate of thinking. Now think this thought, "I am in control of what and how I think." Repeat this phrase in your mind several times. With each repetition become more and more convinced of its truth for your life.

After a moment or two, imagine yourself pressing the pause button on the VCR or DVD player of your mind. Watch the flow of your thought stop. Attempt to hold the non-motion of your thought for three to five minutes. If a thought tries to begin, simply see yourself pressing the pause button again.

Feel the presence of the pause, the presence of the absence of your thinking or worrying about anything at all for this moment in time.

Be limp. Be empty. Be vulnerable and open. Be aware. If there is a thought or idea that passes before you that you don't want to forget, gently note it and return as smoothly as you can to your time of emptiness. Cultivate this practice of being spiritually, mentally, and emotionally still each morning. You are beginning your B.R.E.W.

4. Receiving God's Love

"You will discover that the more love you can take in and hold on to, the less fearful you will become.
—Henri Nouwen, *The Inner Voice of Love*

"In God's bosom is an ocean full of love."
—K.B.J.

The Morning Dip

I once served on the Board of Trustees for a beautiful YMCA facility in Silver Bay, New York. Set on the bountiful banks of Lake George, the retreat center is surrounded by the awesome Adirondack Mountains. The sacrifice for being on the board was traveling to this trying setting four times a year. During one of my first trips, I was enjoying an early morning walk and noticed a group of persons swimming together in the lake. This seemed unusual to me because it was so early in the morning, and it was a large group of ten to fifteen persons. Later on in the day I picked up a schedule and read that the early morning swim was a scheduled communal event known as "The Morning Dip." At the time I could not swim and was unable to participate in the event, but I began practicing my own form of the morning dip. Each morning when I passed the group swimming, I imagined myself swimming, with no small gusto and grace, in those same waters. The image remained with me. Now the waters that I imagine are different: I see myself swimming, sometimes floating and backstroking, in God's restorative and unrelenting affection.

My dip is one way of practicing the second movement of B.R.E.W.: receiving God's love. The greater the emptying in B.R.E.W's first movement, the greater the filling in B.R.E.W.'s second movement.

The Waterfall of God's Love

Once when I was very young I remember not being able to sleep. Yet, I must have drifted off, because my memory of that evening does not have waking world explanation. I remember sitting on the side of the bed and suddenly feeling a liquid substance coming down on my head. I did not look up because I believed the source to be invisible and mysterious. I was not afraid, but was filled with wonder. This experience is perhaps the reason why I have a tender place in my heart for waterfalls, not just the kind that rush down ledges in one mighty flow, but streams falling down a mountain and mist and rain falling from the sky.

I have a small stained-glass picture of a waterfall in my home office. The place where the water is falling is surrounded by purple and white flowers. On some mornings, I imagine myself kneeling inside that picture. I let the water fall on my head and down my back. I feel the tingle as it touches my skin and my soul. There are times when I envision a waterfall of my own creation. The setting is not as important as the rushing water falling down on me. Sometimes I lift my face to a falling stream and smile.

What difference would it make for you to imagine God's love falling freshly on your face every day?

The Importance of Receiving

In John 12:1-8, Jesus is eating with his disciples and receiving the lavish anointing of Mary Magdalene. Judas, under the guise of missionary concern, attempts to end Mary's generous show of affection. Jesus will have none of it. He tells Judas, in essence, to shut up and mind his own business. The role reversal of Jesus as recipient as opposed to giver is significant, and so is the pictorial image. Not only does Jesus accept the role of the receiver, but he reclines into the role, savors it, and resists all attempts to snatch it from him. Jesus seems as used to receiving as he was to giving. I think there was a reason for this. The Gospels record times when Jesus removed himself from both the crowds and his disciples in order to be alone and receive something. That something, I believe, was Godly Acceptance straight from God. Having received love freely, Jesus was able to extend love freely in ways that incensed some and inspired others.

The second element of B.R.E.W., receiving God's love, offers you a chance to take love as it is extended to you by Creator and Creation. I have come to believe this reception is the necessary prerequisite for life as well as service to others. You cannot give what you do not have. Receiving is the unsung gift of the spirit. We place so much emphasis on giving that we fail to comprehend the preeminent value of receiving.

Endless giving without the ability to receive leads to bitterness. I have observed this in pastors; I have lived this as a pastor. I once believed that life was first and foremost about serving others. Such a fixation led to constant energy outflow. While I did not often show it in my interactions with others, many times I felt drained and used. Add ingratitude to the mix and you have a person smiling wide to cover a large emptiness. I was liberated in my life and ministry when I realized that my first calling as a person and minister was not to do anything for anybody. My first calling was to simply receive God's love. This knowledge was so meaningful that it created a healing refreshment that filled me head to toe. And it transformed my giving. Giving from abundance is different from giving from shortage. I gave more freely and joyfully as I experienced God's love more freely and joyfully. I had not only a desire to give, but a compulsion to do so. God's love, genuinely experienced, naturally flows out from you toward others. Why shouldn't this be the case? We are all the outflows of God's magnanimous love.

Receiving and Knowing

Be careful, it is possible to mistake receiving God's love for simply knowing that God loves you. Religious people often repeat scriptures and sing songs that tell us of God's love without really accessing that love. You can know how to vote, be registered to vote, and not ever cast a single ballot. Similarly, millions may know about God's love and be signed up for it on church, mosque, and synagogue membership registers around the world without ever feeling such mighty love afresh and anew. When do you actually grab hold of the divine love that is allegedly yours? When was the last time you let such love grab hold of you? When was the last time you actually felt God loving you in church or anywhere else for that matter? We are persons who live by thoughts and feelings. In fact, the thoughts that are joined with feelings, either positive or negative, are the thoughts that create most of our circumstances and living outcomes. Feelings ignite perceptions and vice versa. Feeling God's love for you is one of the most empowering blessings you can give to yourself.

Morning B.R.E.W. is not about recalling and repeating certain biblical truths to help guide you through your day. Nowhere is this more true than this second phase of morning B.R.E.W. where you are not saying, but sipping God's love. Psalm 34:8 invites us to "taste and see that the Lord is good." B.R.E.W. is about tasting and seeing, not just knowing. Savor God's love; relish it. Feel the love of God filling your being with fresh grace each morning. If you can feel God's love, all the dehumanizing demons of life will not be able to oppress you and hold you back.

Loving God and God Loving You

It is also possible for us to mistake God's love for us with our love for God. Much of our worship is geared to manufacturing rituals of prayer and praise that are sufficient enough to garner God's attention. We want to please God in worship. I dare not challenge such a worthy pursuit, but that's our agenda in worship. What's God up to in worship? Is God just gathering it all in or is God, already more than sufficiently endowed, valiantly trying to get though to us with an ocean full of grace. What if we thought God wanted to please us a zillion times more than we wanted to please God, not because of our sacrifices, but just because? What if worship is more about receiving from God than it is about rendering unto God? What if every day of your life, from now on, you took a moment to simply relax and accept God's acceptance of you? How selfish is it to receive God's love? How selfish is it not to?

How to Receive God's Love

It is time for you to write again. This time I want you to time yourself. For the next five minutes I want you to write as many instances of receiving as you can. I am going to do this exercise also, and I will share with you what I write. Go ahead and begin. Use the space below to list as many instances of receiving as you can. You can list your instances in any way you desire:

After five minutes are up, stop.

During the five minutes I came up with the following:

- child receiving Christmas gift
- graduate receiving diploma
- mailbox receiving mail
- beloved receiving flowers
- ground receiving water
- animals receiving food
- sky receiving rain
- body receiving air
- ground receiving footsteps
- person receiving a ticket
- family receiving bad news
- sky receiving sunshine
- hand receiving touch
- ears receiving voice

Go back and look at your list. What stands out for you? Notice how your list may be reflective of your surroundings and mood. My list reflects the fact that I am sitting in front of our wide living room window, gazing out into a gorgeous summer afternoon sky and landscape. Also, while I was doing the exercise, our youngest child, Jovonna, entered the room and asked me a question. While most of my instances are positive, two are negative, including a citation (I wonder where that came from?) and troubling news. For the purposes of this exercise, I want you to focus on your positive images of receiving.

By doing this exercise you have just made a list of possible ways to imagine receiving God's love. I want you to take a moment to do so right know. Pick one of your positive images. (I will focus on a mailbox receiving mail.) Imagine God as the giver and yourself as the receiver. (God is filling my mailbox with mail!) Once you have selected the image and made the substitutions, close this book and take a minute to ponder the image loosely. Do not force the direction of the image, but allow it to take you where it will. Relax and receive God's love in your mind and heart in a fresh new way.

The Gifts of Receiving God's Love

What does a child get from knowing that he or she is loved? I asked Jovonna this once. She replied with a ready forthrightness that caught me off guard, "It encourages me and it helps me to live." I remember hearing once that the two best things parents can give their children are roots and wings. Receiving God's love strengthens me each day by *rooting* and *releasing* me.

When I think of rooting, an old church song comes to mind:

I shall not, I shall not be moved
I shall not, I shall not be moved
Just like a tree planted by the water
I shall not be moved.[9]

This song is not about stubborn resolve; it is about an empowering, defining connectedness. When I am feeling

God's love, I am receiving confirmation of my place and importance in the universe. Amidst all that there is in the world and cosmos, I am as important as any of it in God's eye. Buoyed by a sacred sense of my spiritual significance, I am less likely to go off on an endless search for acceptance in all the wrong places. Our basic acceptance cannot be found in any place other than God, Ultimate Reality. If Ultimate Reality accepts us, there is no higher or more fulfilling form of acceptance. That solid ground of affection is root worthy; you can be planted there assured of who you are and whose you are.

Confusion about our identity and worthiness sabotages and saps our living force and energy. To be sure, it is a layered draining away of energy. There is the drain of the continuing confusion, the drain of feeling burdened by the confusion, and the drain of energy expended in an attempt to alleviate the confusion. Confusion about our identity and worthiness leaves us aimless and listless. We are, in essence, dead people walking.

Resolution about who we are and whose we are resurrects us. It releases us for the delights and challenges of life. I recall being at the crossroads of one of the toughest decisions of my life. For four years I served as the founding pastor of an extraordinary church in my home city, New Orleans. Beacon Light Baptist Church was an adventure. It began with forty faithful members that included family and friends and, in a very short time, the church was brimming with new members and a contagious vitality. At a zenith point in its success, instead of feeling contentment, I began feeling restless with a new dream. I felt called to enter a

Ph.D. program in the northeast and prepare myself to teach and minister to the church and community in other ways. More and more, I sensed the dream taking me away from my comfort zone. Riddled with anxiety and apprehension, I journeyed to upstate New York for a conference. Before leaving the conference, I remember standing on a high bank overlooking what I believe was the Hudson River. There I prayed for God to show me the way. I did not expect to receive an answer so soon or for the answer to be so satisfying and soothing. I opened my eyes and saw what appeared to be two walking paths reaching outward toward opposite directions. Then these un-thought words sounded in my spirit: "Whatever road you take, I will be with you."

Whoosh! I remember feeling an amazing lightening of load. Being assured that neither choice would cost me God's loving company and blessing, I felt a new easy freedom flow through my veins. On the banks of the river, I was released to own my choice-making capacity as a child of God and to decide with more joy and less burden.

God gives us choices to bless us, not burden us. Assured of God's unconditional company, we are freed to embrace our sacred humanness, which includes imagining and making choices. To access your power of choice is not to negate God's will, it is to live out God's will that you be an adventurous and creative human being. If God wanted to be responsible for it all, God would not have created response-able human beings. Being loved by God frees us to lean into all of our divine attributes and live the best life we can possibly live.

God's Mad Love and Duke Ellington

In my Jazz of Preaching class at Andover Newton Theological School, one of my favorite persons to discuss is Edward Kennedy "Duke Ellington." A pianist, composer, and band leader, Ellington was one of the most prolific jazz artists ever. He composed over two thousand songs, some say closer to three thousand. Among the depths of his musical riches are his classic Sacred Concerts. Ellington's compositional genius can be linked to his experience of rootedness and release.

When he was a child growing up in Washington, D. C., Duke's mother, Daisy Kennedy Ellington, told him repeatedly that he was "God's child." Ellington grew up feeling that he was "a son of God." Ellington recalled his mother telling him, "Edward, you are blessed. You don't have anything to worry about. Edward, you are blessed." There is no stronger belief for a child to have in the impressionable early years of life then the belief that he or she is blessed by God. This rootedness in God's esteem, I believe, was the bedrock of Ellington's legendary creativity. Having freely received, we can freely give, over and over again. Speaking to the audience on behalf of his band members, Ellington concluded every concert with the following words, "We love you madly."

Each morning, find a way to visualize and experience God's mad love for you. Such love will root and release, affirm, heal, and empower you.

When It's Hard to Receive or Conceive God's Love

The April 8, 2002, *U.S. New & World Report* article about the earthquake in Mahrin, Afghanistan, tore away at me, and I suppose many others too.

A woman identified as Shaima rocks on her heels amid mounds of mud-brick rubble and wails a low, mournful refrain. "Oh, my children. Oh, my children." She will not leave this particular pile of earth because this, at least, is hers. And after an earthquake hit her village Monday night, killed four of her children, and flattened her home, this is all she has left. "I don't know what God wants anymore," she says.

Though most of us will never know such despair, most of us have or will come to a point of not feeling God's affection or nearness. John of the Cross, a sixteenth-century Christian writer called this "the dark night of the soul." How do I feel God's love when God seems gone? I sit, hurt, and wait as God sits, hurts, and waits with me unseen in the shadows.

One morning, I lamented my own woes and the troubles of the world. In my grief-making and taking, I began wondering how God could take heartbreak after heartbreak and the cumulative resulting pain, over the vast expanse of time. Silence. And then I saw an image of God's bosom as an ocean of love filled with tears, but even more, filled with life-giving waters sufficient enough to hold, if not wash away, the hurt.

Relentless Presence
God need not
be named or noticed
to be around.
—K.B.J.

Our Tears

Author Frederick Buechner says that we need to pay special attention to "unexpected tears." Early on during my B.R.E.W. experience of feeling God's love, I noticed tears. You may cry as well, depending on the way you are wired. For me, the tears seem to be the result of an overwhelming sense of being held and affirmed. They are joy-tears from being tenderly touched in tender places.

After each writing session, I save my manuscript on my laptop's hard drive and on an external portable hard drive. Once when I was saving to the portable drive, I did hold it in the palm of my hand. I could feel the device vibrating as it stored my writing in a safe place. I could feel the power of this humanly designed and created mechanical device at work. We are spirit beings. Against the backdrop of eternity, we will spend most of our existence as the spirit beings we are. Why shouldn't you feel the power of God's love moving inside you? Why shouldn't you cry?

Remember Who You Are
You are God's beloved child
You are filled with
love, truth, and power
So, be free to
rest and search
receive and lose
rejoice and cry
Knowing that through it all,
there remains
Brilliant Grace.
—*K.B.J.*

5. Embracing Personhood, Humanity, and Creation

"We are addicted to our limited vision of ourselves."
—Kenny Werner, Musician

"Don't leave it to others to define who you are and will become. That's between you and your dreams."
—K.B.J.

"Most of us go to our graves with our music still inside us."
—Oliver Wendell Holmes

"Everybody' got a Hole. Ain't nobody ever lived who don't got a Hole in them somewheres. When I say Hole you know what I'm talking about dontcha? Soft spot, sweet spot, opening, blind spot, Itch, Gap, call it what you want but I call it a Hole."
—Willa Mae Beede in *Getting Mother's Body* by Suzan-Lori Parks

Self-Denial and Self-Affirmation

We either choose to love and grace ourselves and others, Holes and all, or we don't. Note that Suzan-Lori Parks capitalizes "Holes" in the preceding passage. The holes are a part of our

Holy. The provocation and impetus are there, still the choice to love is one we choose or choose not to make each day. Sometimes we don't choose to embrace ourselves actively or at all because we have been taught that such embracing runs counter to the more genuine sacrificial impulses of religious life. The challenge is to rewire what we think about ourselves in relation to the self-denial themes of the Christian faith.

I enjoy giving workshops on self-care based on my first book, *Rest in the Storm: Self-Care Strategies for Clergy and Other Caregivers*. Once, during a workshop discussion, a chaplain voiced distress at attempting to reconcile the self-care message I was presenting with the self-sacrifice motif of the Bible. He mentioned Paul, in particular, as a model of heroic sacrificial living. Authentic faith, in the mind of some, challenges us to be "crucified" with Jesus, to give ourselves to others in unrestricted, unrelenting service.

Perhaps you believe this as well, and thus it is difficult for you to accept a theology that trumpets self-affirmation. I contend that self-denial and self-affirmation are mutually compatible with each other. Indeed, self-denial demands self-affirmation. There can be no self-denial apart from having a self in the first place. Self-denial without a self to begin with is a hoax. It is theologically sound within the Christian tradition to think that you and your individual needs are in concert with your faith commitment and expression. Healthy religion affirms God and God's creation in the same breath.

A theology of self-care and self-affirmation asks the question, "Can you cooperate with God to love yourself toward your best self?" As potent as the love of God is, it can be severely diluted by your unwillingness to love yourself. You sabotage God's love for you when you don't love yourself, effectively rendering God's love null and void in your life.

Watch Heaven Rejoice
Can you stand
living in light?
Can you imagine
sustained joy,
sharpened intuition,
and expanded intelligence?
Can you wield
the sword
of your own brilliance?
Answer, "Yes."
And watch heaven rejoice.
—K.B.J.

Embracing Ourselves through B.R.E.W.

To embrace yourself through B.R.E.W., take some moments to honor who you are as part of your morning ritual. After experiencing stillness and feeling loved by God, follow the natural flow of feeling good about who you are. I say natural flow, because the first two elements of B.R.E.W. will dig a well of positive energy inside you. Direct that energy toward deliberate self-affirmation. Your task is to cultivate thoughts and feelings that bathe you in good will. Visualization is one of the most effective ways to accomplish this.

As you have visualized emptiness and God loving you, now visualize self-acceptance. Feel it. The options are endless. One way to fill your reservoir of possibilities is to think of moments in your life when you have felt fully affirmed and accepted. Remember them and replay them as a way of affirming who you are. Another way to visualize self-embracing is to have a picture of yourself near your B.R.E.W. space. When the moment for embracing comes, simply look at the picture and offer a smile of acceptance and gratitude. As you use a picture to help you embrace yourself, be mindful that the picture may represent you in the past or the present but it will not be a rendering of who you are becoming. Don't over-focus on the picture. Allow it to represent you as you were, are, and are becoming.

Along with visualizing acceptance, affirmations have proved to be transformative for me in this segment of B.R.E.W. Here are a few of my favorite self-affirmations:

I am God's child.
Greatness is my birthright.
I am a child of God's great universe.
I was born to play and soar.
I am God's constant new creation.

I encourage you to develop an extended affirmation, a human rights declaration. Here is one of mine:

I am a child of God, a person who God loves unconditionally.
I will live and laugh, give and grow in God's grace.

It is important that you see this moment of embracing your personhood as sacred as the two prior phases of B.R.E.W., being still and receiving God's love. Religious experience that does cultivate personal health and wholeness is not in your best interest. Good religion celebrates divinity and humanity in the same breath. I believe the early church leader, Irenaeus, was right when he said, "The Glory of God is a person fully alive."

When experienced fully, the "sacred" energy of B.R.E.W. nurtures emotional and psychological energy for living life more abundantly. The Pentecost narrative of Acts was not about a bestowal of energy for being religious, but for living more creatively and powerfully in everyday life. To be filled with the spirit is to be filled with bountiful grace, including thoughts and sensibilities that free us to be and become our best spiritual, emotional, physical, and social selves.

Be Careful of the Self You Embrace

As you embrace yourself, take note of "the you" you are hugging. Each of us has images of ourselves that we don't need to embrace. We need to send those images away. Often we paint ourselves exclusively in the colors of our perceived failures, needs, and wounds. Some people are over-fixated on themselves, consciously or unconsciously, as victims or as wounded ones. As real as our wounds are, over-identifying with our wounds can blind us to the reality of our deepest identity as whole, well children of God with unrestricted spiritual potential.

Over-emphasizing your pains will keep you from one of the most glorious truths of all: It's not what happens that matters, but how you respond to what happens. Your response-power is truly amazing. Paul perceived it in one soulfully ecstatic moment and proclaimed: "I can do all things through him who strengthens me" (Philippians 4:13). Be careful that the self you embrace is not just your wounded self, but your empowered self, equipped to weather the wounds and walk on.

Embrace Your Emerging Self

The Christian faith leans toward change, newness, and transformation. As you practice B.R.E.W., become increasingly comfortable with your continuing self transformation, your evolving self. You can facilitate this by purposefully and intentionally thinking about your emerging self more during your B.R.E.W. self meditation. Pay attention to who you are as a unique child of God with extraordinary powers and potential. Embrace your emerging self, the you, you want to be, the you God is cheering you on to be.

The B.R.E.W. self-embrace moment is a good time to listen to the dreams and desires bubbling up inside you. Thank God for writers like John Eldridge and Erwin Raphael McManus, who have rescued the sacred meaning and value of words and realities like desire and passion. Use B.R.E.W. self-embrace to nurture your God-given desires and passion. Note them, ponder them, and explore them in post-B.R.E.W. journaling sessions.

Connecting with and embracing your emerging self involves growth-aspiration and growth-actualization. First, conceptualize who you are now and who you want to be in terms of traits, skills, and accomplishments. Begin to picture and imagine your growing self, your emerging self. Don't settle for an early version or the present version of who you are. "If anyone is in Christ, there is a new creation." (2 Corinthians 5:17) That newness is not just about a single change in an instant, but about ongoing change over a lifetime. Developing a more active awareness of your growth intention and potential is integrally important, not just professionally, but spiritually. The work of change is holy and God-inspired work. It is the energizing work of dreaming, of imagining. The power to dream and imagine in order to create something new are second only in dynamic potency and vitality to God's power to create. "Where there is no vision," according to Proverbs 2:18, "the people perish" (KJV). That's not just true for nations; it's true for persons.

Leveling Up

When you have a clear vision of who you are now and who you want to be, you can actualize your growth; you can work and rest toward your "leveling up." Those last two words come from the computer video gaming world. One genre of gaming is called RPGs, role playing games. These games allow you to play a character that grows in strength throughout the game. The movement from old strength to new stronger strength is referred to as leveling up. Do you have a sense of yourself leveling up in life?

How do you know you are leveling up? What are your leveling up goals? Do your leveling up goals incorporate every major dimension of your life? How do you evaluate your current level and gauge the distance between where you are and where you want to be? B.R.E.W. self-embrace moments can provide the space for this kind of life-generating thinking. Expect and explore raised levels of awareness, energy, creativity, and wonder. Consciously level up; grow in strength, with purpose and with passion. Give yourself permission to be strong and stronger. Do not fear your strength, but leap toward it. Often at momentous points in Scripture an angel is nearby saying, "Don't be afraid." Usually the potentially threatening reality is the presence and power of God. I have come to see that the angelic enjoinder isn't just applicable to our fear of our awesome God, it is relevant to our fear of our awesome selves.

Greatness Is Your Birthright

In the summer of 2004, America Online ran pictures of athletes Tiger Woods and Venus Williams with the headline, "Are They Has-Beens?" Two superior athletes were thus, momentarily at least, relegated to the trash heap of cultural notoriety because they were no longer winning every event they entered. But is greatness just about winning? Greatness is not about winning at all. Greatness is about imagining new challenges and expanding the perimeters of your power, less in competition with others and more in concert with others. The only person who can determine whether or not you are a has-been or never-was is you. Your greatness is a matter of you and your dreams. Can you stand greatness as a way of life, a living aspiration and norm? Can you embrace greatness, embrace your own creative aspirations and lean into your best strengths, including the strength of vulnerability, as a way of life? I dare you! I double dare you! Jesus did not condemn greatness; he redefined it and then challenged his followers to aspire to ever greater experiences and contributions. Let B.R.E.W. cultivate in you an overwhelming sense of new worth, aspiration, and power. As you feel your life filling and expanding with new possibility and wonder, trust your growth; lovingly embrace the self you are becoming.

The great dancer, Martha Graham, reminds us of the ultimate importance of this holy matter:

> There is a vitality, a life force, an energy, a quickening which is translated through you into action, and because there is only one of you in all time, this expression is unique. And if you block it, it will never exist.[10]

The Great Convergence
You are God's dream, and
  who you dream yourself to be.
You are God's creation, and
  who you create with your beliefs and choices.
You are the result of Insistent Love, and
  what you insist on loving each day.
—K.B.J.

Embracing Others

How much greatness are you willing to grant yourself? How much greatness are you willing to grant others? When you are at home with yourself, you are freed to be more fully at home with others. Embracing yourself will make it more possible to embrace others. Practicing B.R.E.W., in all of its dimensions, has extraordinary social significance, but especially this dimension of embracing others.

You can create a ritual of embracing others in your imagination. After you have honored your self, envision humanity as a whole or picture a group of persons or an individual you know. See them clearly in your mind. Take a moment to bow toward them, gently touch them, shake their hands, and hug them in your spirit. In your imagination, see yourself doing this and feel the sensations of this occurrence. Actively nurture positive sentiments for each of the persons in you have pictured.

This ritual can be particularly helpful in dealing with difficult people. You know them. They spark red in you when they are in your general vicinity. In fact, they don't even have to be nearby. Simply having these people in mind stirs hard feelings inside you. One of the ways to learn how to love such people in life is to practice loving them in your imagination. Use the power of sacred imagination to conjure feelings of grace and goodwill, and then focus this energy toward the difficult people. They may never change (although there is mounting scientific evidence for the invisible power of prayer having potent effects on persons who don't even know they are being prayed for), but you're attitude toward them will have an effect and that can make all the difference in the world. Who knows what will happen when they are affected by your changed attitude? Your changed attitude redefines the interpersonal dynamic, creating the possibility for a positive change in the relationship.

As you take a moment in your morning B.R.E.W. to affirm your humanity by blessing all of humanity, cultivate your capacity for welcoming those who are different. Envision someone significantly different from you and see yourself honoring them in your mind and your heart. Doing so as you practice B.R.E.W. predisposes you to doing so in life. Use your B.R.E.W. practice to melt the barriers of judgment and build bridges of understanding.

Give Someone an "A"

One of the most inspiring books I have ever read is *The Art of Possibility* by Rosamund Stone Zander and Benjamin Zander. Benjamin is a music professor who began the practice of "giving an A" to his students. Instead of having his students strive toward an A or the grade of their choice, Zander gave them an "A" at the beginning of the semester. To keep the grade, students had to write a letter to Zander at the beginning of the semester that explained what they had done that was in keeping with the grade. It was grading by preemptive esteem and educational aspiration. Encouraged by the system's impact on students, Zander suggests that giving an "A" can be a potent social strategy:

> [Giving an "A"] is an enlivening way of approaching people that promises to transform you as well as them. It is a shift in attitude that makes it possible for you to speak freely about your own thoughts and feelings while, at the same time, you support others to be all they dream of being. The practice of giving an "A" transports your relationships from the world of measurement to the world of possibility.[11]

Why not use your B.R.E.W. time to give out "A's" to people who have a tough time measuring up to your standards? While you're at it, give yourself an "A," and dare to live into it. In this way you perform the miracle of rearranging meaning. You open yourself up to exciting, fanciful, and sometimes grueling conversion. Is this not the way, the truth, and the life embodied in and encouraged by Jesus?

Embrace Creation

As caretakers of creation, we should become more sensitive to our ecological realities and challenges. While humans may be the supreme expression of God's love, we certainly are not the only expression of God's love. Use your B.R.E.W. embrace to embrace the world and all therein. Faithfulness includes being faithful stewards of the environment. Such faithfulness begins with honoring nature with our thoughts and beliefs. We are less likely to behave violently and carelessly with a world we know to be as much divine as we are. Indeed, the Genesis account informs us that creation was divine first, and we originate from its original glory.

Nurturing active compassion for creation allows creation to mediate enlightenment and strength to us. As a boy growing up in Florida, Howard Thurman, the future spiritual mentor to thousands, cultivated an organic spirituality in which water, darkness, storms, and an oak tree mediated the presence of God to him in profound and meaningful ways. Thurman writes of the blessing of the oak tree in his magnificent autobiography, *With Head and Heart.* As you read his rapturous words, remind yourself that Thurman has no monopoly on the whisperings of nature. If we display unhindered compassion for God's non-human splendor, we to will be able to hear—and live:

> When the storms blew, the branches of the large oak tree in our backyard would snap and fall. But the topmost branches of the oak tree would sway, giving away just enough to save themselves from snapping loose. I needed the strength of the oak tree, and, like it, I wanted to hold my ground. Eventually, I discovered that the oak tree and I had a unique relationship. I could sit, my back against its trunk, and feel the same peace that would come to me in my bed at night. I could reach down in the quiet places of my spirit, take out my bruises and my joys, unfold them, and talk about them. I could talk aloud to the oak tree and know that I was understood. It, too, was a part of my reality, like the woods, the night, and the pounding surf, my earliest companions, giving me space.[12]

Your B.R.E.W. embrace can be a marvelous morning homecoming of self, others, and creation.

6. Welcoming the Day

"This is the day that the Lord has made; let us rejoice and be glad in it."
—Psalm 118:24

"Every day sing a song of praise, we've come this far by grace, and when you pray to find your place, love will lead the way."
—Brian Blade, *Lead the Way*

"Do you have in your hand or pocket a promissory note guaranteeing that you will be here tomorrow?"
—K.B.J.

I Waked Up! I Welcome the Day

The word *welcome* is derived from words which mean "pleasure" and "come." To welcome the morning or the moment is to believe that life wants to bless, not curse us. Welcoming is turning down suspicion and apprehension for life and turning up expectancy and enthusiasm.

Resist allowing regularity and familiarity with "morning" and "moment" to dull an ongoing attentive thrill for them. What if you were to live as if each morning and every moment was insanely noteworthy? Having a welcoming attitude toward new points in time is a way to cultivate joy for life itself. Welcoming each day moves us from experiencing a mundane life to more meaningful living. In its most dramatic manifestation, welcoming transforms awful existence to awe-filled existence.

When I invite you to welcome the new day, I am asking you to do more than just acknowledge a square with a number on a sheet of paper. I suspect that constantly seeing time pictured as small blocks places unconscious restrictions on our experience of time. As far as eternity is concerned, there is no such thing as blocks of time: yesterdays, todays, and tomorrows. Those are our concocted designations created for human management purposes.

During B.R.E.W. welcoming, imagine the day in seriously fanciful ways. Begin to think about days in ways that invite you to honor them more. In this regard I am always inspired by Frederick Buechner's glorious assessment of "today":

> It is a moment surrounded on all sides by darkness and oblivion. In the entire history of the universe, let alone in your own history, there has never been another just like it and there will never be another just like it again. . . . If you were aware of how precious it is, you could hardly live through it. Unless you are aware of how precious it is, you can hardly be said to be living at all.[13]

In her poem, *Celebration*, Denise Levertov speaks of a day "that shines in the cold like a first-prize brass band swinging along the street."[14] When I encourage you to welcome the new day, I am inviting you to intentionally receive a fresh awareness of God, life, yourself, and others. Welcome a new experience of time, in time. Take a moment to notice your aliveness at another extraordinary point in eternity. Allow the amazement of this truth to fill your being. And, if you dare, be grateful for such a mind-boggling blessing. Against this backdrop, having a good day is almost a given, and having a great day is a possibility better than good.

Will the Real Day Please Stand Up?
That which stands before you
*   is much more than a date.*
A day is a dazzling image
*   of eternity dressed in time.*
An emissary of God offering
*   sacred exploration and emergence.*
—K.B.J.

Welcoming Ways

How many different ways can you think of to welcome the day? I'll begin with ten ways. You match my ten with your ten.

1. Stand up and receive the day with outstretched arms.
2. Hold the day as if it were a new-born baby.
3. Shake the day's hand.
4. Kiss the day.
5. Hug the day.
6. Bow before the day.
7. Wash the day's feet. Foot-washing is an ancient action of hospitality.
8. Offer a Declaration of Welcome
9. Greet the day as a friend arriving at the airport, train station, or bus depot.

10. See the oncoming day as a child sees a parade coming down the street or the circus coming into town.

List your ten ways to welcome the day.

1.

2.

3.

4.

5.

6.

7.

8.

9.

10.

Add one more for the fun of it!

11.

Handling the Fire of Creation

Once, while writing a note for this book, my pen began to write lighter. I followed an urge to hold the tip of the pen close to a candle I was burning. Sure enough, the warmth of the fire coaxed down some hardened, contrary ink still left in the pen. In welcoming the day you must not be afraid to approach new fire. It will call forth a new flow of sacred energy.

Part of welcoming the day is welcoming your part in creating the day. God's role is with things we have no power over, such as events and circumstances out of our control, and God's good and bountiful grace. Moreover, we do not have any control, as for as we know, over those supra-rational, intuitive, and unconscious thoughts and ideas that flood our inner world, impacting reality in subtle, hidden ways. God and the knowledge beyond our everyday-in-our-head beliefs and understandings are mighty creative forces on our lives. But they aren't the only realities God has deemed to form what happens and does not happen.

Part of the Genesis dominion allocation of creation is the ability to design our lives with the thoughts we think. As divine offspring of Loving Mysterious Creativity, we can think and feel reality into earthly existence. Jesus kept talking about the kingdom as being something that is inside of us. Our power to create is, in part, what Jesus was referring to. Part of welcoming the day is welcoming your participation in creating the dynamic development and trajectory of each new day. Not only are we children of God, but by God's decree we are also co-creators with God. Every morning is a blank page awaiting your thoughts, beliefs, and actions. What will you paint today? Or what will you burn into existence with your thoughts, feelings, intentions, and the sanctified force of follow-through.

Have an Adventure of a Day

Our third child, Joya, spent an academic year in France. During her pre-flight orientation, I was especially challenged by one of the presenter's remarks. He encouraged this group of high school students, who were setting out for various spots around the world, to open themselves up to the adventure of it all. He warned them against using cell phones and the Internet as a way to bring the familiar to their new experience. He encouraged them to disconnect as much as possible with the familiar, and to open up as completely as they could to their educational and social experience in a different country. His advice triggered something inside me. When it comes to adventures, attitude is more important than location. With the wrong attitude, an excursion to the farthest and most exotic locale on the planet can miss igniting the spirit.

As you begin intentionally welcoming each day, you will experience excitement for the day growing. You will begin to see in fresh new ways that each day holds the promise for marvelous enchantment and fulfillment at work and leisure. A welcoming attitude will develop a wellspring of creative energy for the day.

The most important factor in determining whether or not your day will be an adventure filled with love, search, risk, challenging labor, and heartfelt leisure is your attitude. Think ordinary, and ordinary will be your lot. Think exceptional, and that expectation will drive you toward its fulfillment with faithful vigor and zest.

The blessing of Jesus, I am sure, was that he gave each day new "oomph" and "gusto." When people were with him, they felt alive in ways they had never felt before. He was not so much interested in life after death as some of his followers have been throughout the ages, but rather life before death. Life before death involves making the days matter with deep meaning, purpose, and passion. The adventuresome spirit I have in head and heart is manifested well in the following explosive prose by Diane Ackerman:

> The great affair, the love affair with life, is to live as variously as possible, to grow one's curiosity like a high-spirited thoroughbred, climb aboard, and gallop over the thick hills every day. Where there is no risk, the emotional terrain is flat and unyielding and, despite all its dimensions, valleys, pinnacles, and detours, life will seem to have none of its magnificent geography, only a length. It began in mystery, and it will end in mystery, but what a savage and beautiful country lies in between.[15]

Welcome the morning and then seek to make it an adventuresome day. Place a sanctified exclamation point at the beginning of your day.

September 11

I am writing this on September 11, 2004. Three years ago today, American innocence and sense of security were shattered, as persons and buildings collapsed in sudden, shocking death and destruction. Such mammoth loss is now rightfully carved into the consciousness of our nation. The eleventh day of September will never come and go again without someone, somewhere remembering. Yet even as we respect the dead with affection and memory, I sense somehow that we need to reclaim the date.

That the September 11 date is now cloaked with vial evil troubles my spirit. The date itself has become synonymous with the diabolical deed. Perhaps some of this could not be avoided, given that almost immediately persons and media began referring to the deed and the date in the same breath. Of course, the date had nothing to do with the deed.

Is it right to burden all of the September 11's to come with the burden of September 11, 2001? Can we allow future September 11's to be what they will be on their own terms? Or is the day and date forever scarred? If so, we will never be able to truly welcome the date again; we will miss the promise and blessing of the magical, majestic September 11's in waiting.

We miss the promise and blessing of any days and dates that we consciously and unconsciously do not live anew. What other dates in your life hold special meaning for you? Do you look forward to or regret the arrival of their anniversaries? Maybe that's the point; each day is more than an anniversary, either good or bad. Each new day is a new, innocent entity, waiting for us to live it through in manifold ways. Even as we remember, we need to resist over-marking *this* day with *that* day.

Welcoming the day means not letting anything, including unbelievable evil, blind us to the wonder of each new day, whatever the date. We do well to repeat David's decree in Psalm 118:24, "This is the day which the Lord has made; let us rejoice and be glad in it."

The Dance

Mystery

> *Knowledge*

Surrender

> *Willfulness*

Darkness

> *Light*

Trust
Partners
Steps
Exchanges

> *Dips and*

> *Swings*

Dance on, dance on, dance on

> *down*

> > *the road.*

—K.B.J.

Wow Wells

Is it wrong to believe that life can be an adventure everyday,
that each day can be filled with
wonder and enchantment?

Is it a mistake to feel that the best day we have ever lived
is the one we are currently living,
or tomorrow?
Why do we settle for mundane existence?
Why do we accept as given,
whatever we are given?

Why don't we imagine more adventures,
take more journeys,
mix more wild meaning for ourselves?

We need a vision of life as grandest invitation!

Maybe the appeal of so-called "reality" television shows
          is an indication
of how thirsty we are for life
as more than we usually know it to be.
The trouble is that such a vital thirst can only
          be squelched,
never fully quenched,
by gulping down the antics of others.
What about digging and drinking from
your own wow wells
of whimsical challenge and change?
—K.B.J.

7. The Benefits
of B.R.E.W.

"Weeping may linger for the night, but joy comes with the morning."
—Psalm 30:5

"And suddenly from heaven there came a sound like the rush of a violent wind, and it filled the entire house where they were sitting."
—Acts 2:2

"You don't have to wait until you get to heaven to experience heavenly things."
—K.B.J.

The more I practice morning B.R.E.W. the more I notice that I am experiencing ten distinct benefits. Almost every day I experience a new personal freedom and new energy and power for living. I have greater clarity about my life and the direction I want to go. My creativity is nurtured, and I have a deep sense of joy and connectedness to all of life. I have a greater capacity to hold tension and grieve without despair. I experience peace, mindfulness, and contentment as a sacred residue that covers and permeates me, and I find that I want to give testimony to the beauty and blessing I feel. Let me share just a little bit more about each of these benefits of practicing morning B.R.E.W.

Personal Freedom

This poem best expresses the sense of personal freedom that is growing in me each day.

> **Freedom Welcome**
> *Single tear forms and falls*
> *upon receiving*
> *newest invitation*
> *to behold morning radiance.*
>
> *And, to be rid of*
> *any damnable thing*
> *that dares to hinder*
> *the free soaring of my soul.*
> —K.B.J.

Living Energy and Power

Over a span of several years, I experienced a lesson in contrast that I will never forget. During this period of time, I dropped our teenagers off at the local high school around 7:15 A.M. and our elementary student off at her school about an hour or so later. The difference in the energy displayed by the older and younger students was striking. Some of the teens appeared to be walking in their sleep. On the other hand, the younger students were wide-eyed, frolicking, and eager. What happens to us as we grow up? Life. Do we have to let life sap us of the enthusiasm for life that most of us had in some portion, at some point, during our early days on the planet?

No. As we age we do not need to lose our enthusiasm for life. But considering the adult stressors that are constantly draining us, our resistance must be purposeful and intentional. We have to choose to be reenergized. We have to create and tenaciously practice rituals that will revive us from within. I have found B.R.E.W. to be a great energizer. My renewal of energy begins in the moment before the practice as I anticipate what the ritual will reveal that day. By the time the ritual is done, while I may not be doing cartwheels, I am usually soulfully alert and mindfully engaged. Connecting to source realities in intimate ways will send currents of spiritual energy through your body. You will be filled with the raw substance we all need to fulfill life's callings to desire, to choose, to journey, to wait, and to dare. For these motions and more, we need energy and we need power.

Power is not a bad word. Filled with negative associations to power, and fanned and fueled by abusive uses of power, many people cannot permit themselves to be filled with sacred energy. Being empowered is our birthright. Can you imagine yourself living powerfully in the most enlivening and liberating sense of the word? Imagining and owning your power is a way to experience sacred, soulful resurrection every day.

As I write this, it is raining outside. Being truly empowered is not about reigning; it is about opening yourself up and receiving God's rain of love and grace for your life, for all life. Guess what? It is raining; I mean it is absolutely pouring, all the time.

Clarity

Focus and openness are vital parts of B.R.E.W. Practicing focus and openness day after day, even for brief periods of time, will develop a B.R.E.W. consciousness that affords greater clarity, direction, and life. Simply put, as you practice B.R.E.W. you will see and understand more. In particular I have found that my dreams are becoming more venturous and my reflections on my dreams are becoming more enlightening. Let me share one memorable experience about three dreams and my B.R.E.W. interpretation and reflection the next morning as recorded in this journal entry:

Dream

Caught in the throes of transitional wrestling, I had three dreams last night. In the first dream, I was seated with someone in a car outside a building. Soon, I saw an elderly male emerge. His face showed that he had lived a very long time and a very long time ago. As I continued to look at the man, I sensed that I had seen him before. Suddenly, I connected him to having been a contemporary of my great-grandparents, Peter and Elizabeth Fields. The realization enlivened me. Gleefully, I spoke up. Referring to my brothers, I started reminding the known stranger of "the four little boys" who had visited my grandparents. His demeanor indicated that he didn't need any coaxing or convincing, he knew who I was.

Who was this man, in fact? Why did I see him in my dream? What was this dream trying to tell me? What is it trying to tell me still?

Reflection
The past comes calling

Past matters

Ah, what was!

Deeply moved

Move on.

Dream
In the second dream, I was standing with someone outside a small house that I felt compelled to enter. The camera in the dream focused on a key I held in my hand. I do not know how I came to have the key. Placing the key into the lock, I opened the door. I entered a museum of a room that appeared to be unlived in. The dream ended.

Was I to inhabit this room? Was it enough to notice the room and keep moving? What did the room represent? What did I see? What didn't I see?

Reflection
New opportunities make their offering to us
We make our offerings, or not, to new opportunities
Where there is no life, three choices confront us:
Abide in lifelessness, make life, or
Move on.

Dream

In the third and final dream, I remember being with someone beside a small boat. We un-lodged the boat, pushed it toward the water, and got in. We came upon a new shore. I protested that the new place did not appear to be the desired destination. The person with me did not argue. We turned the boat around and started back. As we approached our original starting place, two more paths were open before us. The dream ended before I could choose a new direction or while waiting for me to choose a new direction.

Was the journey taken in the dream a mistake? Do all journeys matter, no matter where they take us? Do all choices matter? Is any choice completely right or totally wrong?

Reflection

How faithful is it to turn back
because the land ahead
looms unfamiliar?
Move on.

I notice a comforting, common denominator about the dreams: In each of them I was accompanied; I was never alone.

Never alone
No, never alone
Move on.

Openness and focus will bring you greater clarity.

Creativeness

One of my favorite words is *creativity.* Jazz has made me a student of creativity. My understanding of creativity has broadened to say the least. I used to think of it as a sort of narrow enchanted stream to which only the favored few had access. Now I know creativity is a vast and limitless ocean. If you can't see the ocean, that's because you are in it! Creativity surrounds us all the time. It is the ebb and flow of time and eternity. Theologian Gordon Kaufman takes things even further proposing that "we think of God as the serendipitous creativity throughout the cosmos."[16] I have no trouble whatsoever conceding the link between creativity and divinity.

Creation is the overflow of God's boundless love. It even stands to reason that the closer we draw to God and ourselves as children of God the more our creative nature will shine through and the more we will expect our creative nature to be visible.

As you practice B.R.E.W., notice the ways it frees, deepens, and opens you. Befriend these new feelings; lean into them; baptize your labor in them. New creative fire will be yours. Do not be afraid; love the flame.

Joy

I smile when I recall that Jesus's ministry began at a wedding feast and ended with a fish-fry social. How on earth did we allow Christianity to become so suspicious of living joy?

Joy is deeper than happy-gladness. Joy does not have to smile or laugh to be itself. Joy does not have to act out or announce its presence. Joy is an entrenched sense of all-is-better-than-well-ness. Joy is the overflow of divine and personal acceptance. It is the knowledge and satisfaction of feeling connected to all of life. It is the residue of knowing that a magnificent, miraculous life is your birthright.

Greater Capacity for Holding Tension

Change and growth produce tension, sometimes great tension. But this is positive tension without which we are confined to staying who we are, where we are. Perhaps the main reason why we stay close to the known is the discomfort created by the unknown. Anthony de Mello once suggested that it's not the unknown that upsets us most, but, rather, the loss of the known. In his popular book, *Transitions*, William Bridges discusses a trying place in the middle of all life changes, the neutral zone:

> We need not feel defensive about this apparently unproductive time-out at turning points in our lives, for the neutral zone is meant to be a moratorium from the conventional activity of our everyday existence. . . . In the apparently aimless activity of our time alone, we are doing important inner business.[17]

B.R.E.W. is an ideal strategy for sitting with change and all of its accompanying ambivalence, fear, and anxiety. The alternative is unacceptable. Avoiding the necessary discomfort of change is a prescription for mental, emotional, and spiritual death before we actually die. Thus we are challenged to develop a greater capacity to honor and hold tension, to make it through the bumps and bruises of change and growth. B.R.E.W.'s silence, reflection, and grace mediate space for sitting with the troubling thoughts that sit within us. B.R.E.W. allows us to converse with our doubts and fears and to wait them out, until change has its rightful way with us. B.R.E.W. cultivates what Ellen Langer refers to as "soft vigilance" in hard times. What amazing breakthroughs await us on the backside of tension, paradox, and struggle.

Greater Capacity for Grieving Without Despairing

I am writing this after viewing an online report of funerals being held in Russia. Almost three hundred persons were killed a few days ago in a terrorist act that targeted children. One girl was shot forty-six times. The online presentation focused on grieving parents and family members, some of them mourning the dead they have found and others the ones still missing. It was too hard to watch. Yet it was harder turning away. We are tied together; we are one humanity. Grief tells us so. So I watched and grieved. I grieved, but I consciously held despair at arms length. If I—if we—allow despair to take up residence inside of us, it will be harder to feel the hope, that substance that in the end will lead us all out and home.

Sacred Residue

One day I noticed a sparkling substance on my daughter's face. As I rubbed it off, she tried to recall where she might have picked it up. She could not remember, but the proof that she had picked up something from somewhere was on her face. B.R.E.W. will leave its residue. Long after your morning devotional B.R.E.W. time is over, you will have traces of peace, mindfulness, and living joy left over. These are inner traces that cannot and should not be wiped away. Moreover, B.R.E.W.'s traces are cumulative. The attentiveness, love, esteem, and gratitude you nurture daily will add up. Over time you will become a more attentive, loving, confident, and delightful person. As you develop a B.R.E.W. spirit, you will become more inclined to savor the peace that graces your day, and will seek to become a more active and reactive peace-maker.

Contentment

Contentment means being at home in your own house. It means leaning into and relaxing into who you are. It means trusting who you are becoming.

Testimony

During my youth at Mt. Hermon Baptist Church in New Orleans, the first Sunday of each month was Communion Sunday. Before persons participated in the Lord's Supper they were invited to "testify," to briefly state their commitment to the faith (their determination) and how God had blessed them (their testimony). B.R.E.W. will supply you with many testimonies. Here is one of mine:

Journal Entry, January 20th
I am nearing the end of my B.R.E.W.
and I feel very blessed.
Brilliant sunlight in my window.
Watching snow fall from tree limbs.
Puffs of smoke from a candle.
Beautiful music and waterfall in my ears.
Paying attention to every dimension of my B.R.E.W.
Feeling the power of being able to still my mental flow
of anxieties.
Imagining angels dressed as clowns dumping bucket after
bucket of God's liquid unconditional love on me.
Thankful for the joy, the levity of the God experience—
owning it.
[Religion needs more laughter.]
Feeling awake, attuned, alert.
Feeling grateful.
Feeling Freed.
Feeling on Fire.

8. B.R.E.W. Step-by-Step

Drinking B.R.E.W.

As you begin your practice of drinking B.R.E.W. it will be helpful to follow these steps. As time goes on you will develop your own ritual, your own practice. These steps were very helpful to me when I started and I believe they will guide you as well.

1. Decide on a time frame.

I have had amazing brief and extended experiences. Begin with a time frame that works and feels most comfortable for you. I would recommend beginning with an eight-to-twelve-minute experience, brief enough not to make you overly anxious about it and long enough to allow the experience to touch you in a meaningful way. If you like, use a timer and set it to ring after three minutes at the end of each of the four B.R.E.W. phases. After a while the B.R.E.W. phases will flow naturally into each other. Don't worry about making sure you spend the exact amount of minutes in each phase. Every time you sip B.R.E.W. the experience will be different. Part of the difference will be inspired by the varying lengths of time you spend in each phase.

2. Sit in a comfortable place and, if you are of a mind to, light a candle.
You may also find it helpful to have soothing music playing in the background. Create your mood and setting your way. One size doesn't fit all.

3. Be still.
Become limp and loose in mind, body, and soul. (Remember the lady in the rocking chair.) Your goal is to not think about anything at all. In order to get there you may visualize an image of emptiness, such as an empty house, container, clear sky, or water. Once you have imaged emptiness, let your consciousness free-fall into it. Allow your mind to lay dormant for the time you have planned. Be still. Be open. Be free.

4. Receive God's love.
As your mind, body, and soul are relaxed and well in stillness, begin to acknowledge a loving presence. Allow yourself to be loved by God. An image of God loving you may arise in your spirit. See if you can stay with that image; see it through and receive its blessing for you. You may want to gently conceptualize your own image of God affirming you. Do so in an unforced way. Don't just think, feel God's love. Tears may come, let them.

5. Embrace personhood and creation.
Allow affirmation for yourself, others, and creation to flow out from your feelings of being unconditionally and lavishly loved by God. Give the same feelings to yourself, others, and

creation that God just gave to you a few moments ago. You may speak this affirmation aloud or in your heart. You may choose to picture it in some way. Feel the genuineness of your choice to bless yourself, others, and God's creation.

6. Welcome the morning (or moment).

Filled with the sentiment and rush of sacred enthusiasm (*en theos* means "in God"), greet the onset of the day (or the moment if you are drinking B.R.E.W. at another time). Open your spirit up to the promise and opportunity that new life holds. Imagine greeting the morning or moment in a fine, if not fiery, way. Give passion; take joy.

7. Voice a prayer of thanks.

As you finish your B.R.E.W., you may want to enter into a period of reflection or—even better—journal about your B.R.E.W. experience, important experiences, or decisions in your life. B.R.E.W. places you in a mindset for greater clarity and understanding. B.R.E.W. taps your rational, intuitive, and imaginative powers. While such powers are keenly on and active, bring them to bear on a challenge or problem you are facing.

Oh yes, there is one other rather important recommendation: If you have lit a candle, please don't forget to blow it out. As for you, keep burning!

B.R.E.W. Variations

1. A single taste; focus on one segment.

Sometimes during B.R.E.W. you will be inspired to extend a particularly meaningful segment of the experience. If you are on a tight schedule this will mean less time for the other segments of B.R.E.W. Here is a solution: just don't include the other segments during that B.R.E.W. session. Savor the singular taste of the single segment of being still, receiving God's love, embracing your personhood, or welcoming the day. Believe me, swimming in God's love can be sufficiently empowering by itself. So as you need or decide to, feel free to taste your B.R.E.W. in singular, larger, longer portions.

2. Select different times of day.
It may be that early in the morning doesn't work for you. No problem, drink B.R.E.W. when it's best for you to do so. Remember, drinking it earlier on in the day gives you more time to live with its energizing effects. Also, when not sipped in the morning simply shift element four (welcoming the morning) to welcoming the moment or the time of day you happen to be in. Even after you have established a regular B.R.E.W. time, occasionally have B.R.E.W. at a different time. Different times find us with different attitudes and in different moods. Experiment with B.R.E.W. in a variety of moods. This will make for a richer and more diverse B.R.E.W. experience overall.

3. Try different lengths of time.
While thirty minutes is my B.R.E.W. norm, I have sipped B.R.E.W. for as short as a minute or two, and as long as an hour or so. The experience has always been meaningful and valuable in some way. I have never concluded a B.R.E.W. experience and wished I had spent my time doing something else. B.R.E.W., however, will not always

leave you reeling in ecstasy. Most times, in some way, you will feel new positive energy for living. Longer duration of time is not the lone factor in determining the quality and impact of your experience. I have experienced times when a couple of intensely focused minutes have yielded enormous energy.

Remember spirituality is not just about our thirsting and hungering efforts, but about God's grace. If you are in the right heart place at the right moment something deeply moving can happen to you—in an instant.

Longer periods of time do have their benefits. When you give yourself thirty minutes to an hour for B.R.E.W., you are less likely to be overly time-conscious. You can relax fully in the moment and engage B.R.E.W. at a more deliberate, savoring pace. The longer session also allows you to be more expansive and experimental with your visualizations and affirmations. You don't have to settle for one visualization or affirmation per B.R.E.W. phase; you can play with and be blessed by a vast assortment of presentations.

4. Mix the order of the segments of B.R.E.W.

Though mixing the order will disturb the acronym, try alternating the different segments of B.R.E.W. For instance, reverse the order: welcome the day, embrace personhood and creation, receive God's love, and then be still (W.E.R.B.). Heading toward stillness instead of starting there might even feel more natural to you. Play with B.R.E.W. in this way, paying attention to the different experiences you have with different arrangements. E-mail me some of your testimonies at www.brewseries.com.

5. Get physical.

Though I recommend sipping B.R.E.W. seated, the fact is that I have sipped B.R.E.W. while walking and jogging, including the stillness segment. You can be physically moving and still observe stillness of mind and heart. Even if you do not drink all segments of B.R.E.W. during physical exercise, be open to how you might observe some of B.R.E.W. segments as you move your body.

6. Skip a day or two.

If we are not careful, we can become overly dependent on worthy realities. B.R.E.W. is no exception. B.R.E.W. is a potent spiritual discipline, among many potent life-affirming and life-giving disciplines. Be open to practicing other forms of sacred self-empowerment. Don't grieve days when, either by choice or circumstance, you have not had your B.R.E.W. that day. Allow the days you miss to stir up gratitude for the noticed loss and the anticipation for the next adventure. Also, I have found that an extra potent B.R.E.W. can carry you through more than a day. Sometimes you will experience an aftertaste weeks later.

As you can see, B.R.E.W. is a step-by-step spiritual discipline, but it is also very flexible. As you practice B.R.E.W., make it your own. Your mind, your body, and your spirit will guide you. Don't be burdened by B.R.E.W.; be freed by it. Play with it!

9. B.R.E.W. Extras:

Exploration and Exercise

"Be explorers all your life."
—Stanley Kunitz

"A great many people think they are thinking when they are merely rearranging their prejudices."
—William James

My morning B.R.E.W. has changed my life, but it is not the only thing that has changed me. I have two other morning rituals—exploration and exercise—that help to insure that I have had an adventure or two before nine o'clock every morning. I have learned not to depend on an institution, job, relationship, or any other external reality, no matter how wonderful, to provide the element of excitement in my life. I have learned that I must make my own adventure, morning after morning, day after day. Each morning I engage in exploration and exercise. Often B.R.E.W. informs each of these activities in unexpected and unusually powerful ways.

Exploration

I have an obsession. I don't want a day to go by without learning something new. One of my favorite quotes is a compliment paid to Duke Ellington by Stanley Crouch. He said, "[Ellington] was unable to remain an earlier version of himself. Ellington himself confirms this tendency towards newness. When asked to offer his favorite of his over 2,500 compositions, his response was always the same, 'My next one.'"[18]

I want to learn as many new things as I can each day. Behind this endeavor is a fear of boredom. Someone once said that boredom was the worst sin the church could commit. That may well be true. For my part, boredom is not an option. By boredom, I mean a complicit relationship with the overly familiar and uninteresting. To avoid this malady, I am tenaciously insistent on cutting boredom off at the pass.

One of my strategies for doing this is having a time of morning exploration just after my B.R.E.W., while I am feeling spiritually and mentally alert and open. Morning exploration may be as brief as five minutes or as long as an hour or more. During this time my goal is simple: to put something new in my head. Newness is an assault on boredom. Newness is the doorway to growth and transformation. It is the way we insure that we do not deep freeze ourselves into an earlier version of ourselves. Filling my mind with new information is a way of warding off mental stagnation and ideological entrenchment. We have to work at this; fixation and familiarity are comfortable, possibly deadly.

Here are a few of my favorite morning explorations:

1. Astronomy Picture of the Day

As often as I can, I try to visit http://antwrp.gsfc.nasa/apod/astropix.html. This site presents a new picture of the heavens each day, with an accompanying explanation and additional links for continued research. This fascinating site helps me to keep a big perspective about it all. These striking images also have a way of inflating dreams and diminishing barriers.

2. Poetry Daily

Many mornings, I visit www.poems.com/today.htm. I once said in class, in the inspiration of the moment: "The dancers, the clowns, and the poets will save us." They have saved me; that's for sure. And they keep saving me from surety, over-calculation, and dread.

3. CD Encyclopedias and other Educational Disks

I do not want to leave new knowledge to chance nor do I want to engage the unfamiliar with a mind worn and torn by the challenges of the day. So my morning explorations include digesting an article from Encarta, Encarta Africana, and other modern evangelists of things that I do not know. This endeavor, like running, is a remembering experience for me. I am a reader by genes (according to my mother, my maternal grandmother, Madgie Carter, read herself to sleep) and by choice. One way I quenched my reading thirst as a child and teenager was to randomly read *World Book Encyclopedia* articles. I was and am insatiably curious. We all are in our own ways. I have heard it said that Neil Armstrong, the first human to walk on the moon, said that "it is our instinct to explore." Jesus said, "Ask, and it will be given you; search, and you will find; knock, and the door will be opened for you" (Matthew 7:7).

4. Stretch Books and Periodicals2

Another of my favorite morning explorations is to read a book or journal in a field that takes me beyond the areas of my expertise. Stretch reading feeds me healthy, invigorating doses of the different, prodding me to apprehend and understand in novel, often threatening ways.

Let me take this moment to announce the first inductees in my Stretch Reading Hall of Fame. I present to you four life-giving books and one life-enhancing periodical.

By the Light of My Father's Smile by Alice Walker

Walker writes memorably of how easy it is to have the life sucked out of us by allegedly holy things.

If You Want to Write by Brenda Ueland

This book unleashed my writing spirit. It has done the same for countless others.

Free Play: Improvisation in Life and Art
by Peter Nachmanovitch

Nachmanovitch gave me the courage and rationale to reclaim the first job we ever had: play-makers.

Blessing the Boats by Lucille Clifton

The poets will save us, and this poet will be in the first line of holy wordsmiths. Her poetry is honestly and beautifully well done.

JazzTimes Magazine

I have read more enlightening quotes in this magazine than any other, including those magazines of a theological nature.

5. Journaling

I began journaling when I left my first senior pastorate, Beacon Light Baptist Church in New Orleans. The experience of founding and nurturing a church from its infancy had been exciting and memorable. Through journaling, I intended to hold onto the memories, and reflect on successes and failures. Not long into my efforts, I began writing about things other than Beacon Light. Suddenly my journal became a place to express feelings, ponder decisions, pray, and dream. That was more than two decades ago. Ever since, journaling has been an indispensable tool for cultivating a reflective, purposeful life. More than anything else, I appreciate journaling for helping me to be me and for giving me a place to speak and hear my voice uncut and unedited.

I encourage you to create your own morning exploration ritual. Make your ritual even more meaningful by purchasing a notebook and writing a few notes summarizing your most significant new findings and questions. Pay attention to how your discoveries enhance your thinking and living in everyday life.

Morning Exercise

I either jog or walk four to six days a week. In addition, three days a week I work with weights. Several influences inform my commitment to exercise. First, I was physically active when I was young. Football was the first real passion I had in my life; I loved the game so much. The only thing that could beat the thrill of watching the players run to glory on the gridiron was running like the wind in real life. Oh yeah! Over the past six years, my establishment of an exercise regimen has been, in fact, a remembering of my early love for inspiring physical exertion.

Second, I saw my father die. Frederick Jesse Jones, my champion passed away on October 28, 1998. The week prior to his death, I sat with him, I turned him over, I shaved him, I washed him, and I watched him die. I will never forget that he died with courage. Though initially jolted by the news that he only had a few months to live, my dad regained his living stance and proceeded to die with noteworthy awareness and dignity. I said in his eulogy, "Daddy leaned into his death, asking only that the Lord would 'have mercy' and ease his discomfort." I not only witnessed my father's spiritual strength in death, but the real deterioration of his physical body. I was humbled by the visible fact that my father's stalwart frame could be struck down by sickness and eventually death. I left his deathbed with a new respect for my own body and a resolve to do better by it.

Finally, I exercise because I like the way body, mind, and spirit converge during physical activity. I had an absolutely stunning experience with this one summer morning. Earlier that morning during my B.R.E.W., I had imagined my spirit soaring with the birds as part of my waking up ritual. The image of myself as a spirit remained with me. As I continued to reflect I was reminded, so it seemed, that I was spirit before I became body and will be spirit once I leave body. "Spirit," I heard, "is your first and lasting essence." Think about it, against the backdrop of eternity, the time we spend in our bodies is but a moment.

Well, wouldn't you know it, the spirit words came back as I jogged that morning. It was a day that I was scheduled to run a bit farther than I had been running the prior week. As I came upon the extension point, I felt inspired to imagine my spirit being out in front of me already running toward and already arriving at my destination. I visualized myself achieving my goal by viewing my spirit as already having achieved it. I simply followed my spirit. I ran farther that day than I ever had before and felt playground joy about it. Body, mind, and spirit together, now that's a party!

As I close this book I leave you with a charge, a declaration, and a benediction.

Charge
Build and visit often
an inner sanctuary
where your worries
cannot reach you.

When you leave
your inner space of peace
your worries will not have changed,
but you will have.

Day Break Declarations

I am calm
I am loved by God
I love myself
I love and am loved by others
I have the peace of acceptance.

I am curious
Where will the day take me?
Where will I take the day?
What newness will I come across?
I have the wonder of adventure.

I am excited
New life fills me
New potential rises in and about me
New roads beckon my steps
I have the fire of anticipation.
—K.B.J.

Benediction

May your B.R.E.W. ritual
nourish an abiding B.R.E.W. spirit,
enabling you
to play and soar
from earth to bright glory.
—K.B.J.

A Personal Request

I sense that thousands of persons the world over will have life-changing experiences with *Morning B.R.E.W.* I would very much like to hear from you about the ways B.R.E.W. has made a difference in your life. Please take a moment to write a B.R.E.W. testimony and e-mail it to me through the contact form on one of my Web sites: www.kirkbjones.com, www.brewseries.com, and www.savoringpace.com. Thank you.

—K.B.J.

Notes

1. David Whyte, *Crossing the Unknown Sea: Work As a Pilgrimage of Identity* (New York: Riverhead Books, 2001), 187.
2. Martin Luther King Jr., *The Words of Martin Luther King Jr.* (New York: Newmarket Press), 21.
3. Howard Thurman as quoted in James Melvin Washington, *Conversations with God: Two Centuries of Prayers by African Americans* (New York: HarperCollins, 1994) 182.
4. Shakti Gawain, *Creative Visualization* (Novato, California: Nataraj Publishing, 1978), 11.
5. Liu Chi Kung, as quoted in Jordan Ayan, *Aha!: 10 Ways to Free Your Creative Spirit and Find Your Great Ideas* (New York: Three Rivers Press, 1997), 243.
6. "Where Silence Sends Word," interview with Gillian Conoley by Kevin Larimer, *Poets & Writers Magazine* Jan/Feb 2001, 32.
7. Tilden Edwards, "Living the Day from the Heart," in *Living with God in the Word*, John S. Mogabgab, ed. (Nashville: Upper Room Books, 1993), 59.
8. Bill Milkowski, "Still Searching: Miroslav Vitous Returns with Cut 'N' Paste Syncopations," *JazzTimes*, December 2003, 37.

9. Author unknown, *I Shall Not Be Moved.*

10. Martha Graham, Laura Moncur's Motivational Quotations, www.quotationspage.com.

11. Rosamund Stone Zander and Benjamin Zander, *The Art of Possibility*, (Boston: Harvard Business School Press, 2000), 26.

12. Howard Thurman, *With Head and Heart,* (New York: Harcourt Brace Jovanovitch, 1979), 8-9.

13. Frederick Buechner, *Listening to Your Life* (San Francisco: Harper, 1992), 234.

14. Denise Levertov, *This Great Unknowing: Last Poems* (New York: New Directions Books, 1999), 5.

15. Diane Ackerman, *A Natural History of the Senses* (New York: Vintage Books, 1991), 309.

16. Gordon Kaufman, *In the Beginning . . . Creativity* (Minneapolis: Fortress Press, 2004), xiii.

17. William Bridges, *Transitions: Making Sense of Life's Changes* (New York: Addison-Wesley Publishing Company, 1980), 114.

18. Stanley Crouch, "Duke Ellington: Jazz Artist of the Century," *JazzTimes* (December 1999).

About the Author

A native of New Orleans, Louisiana, Dr. Kirk Byron Jones is the son of Ora Mae Jones and the late Frederick Jesse Jones. He is married to Mary Brown-Jones of Boston, and they are the parents of Jasmine, Jared, Joya, and Jovonna Jones.

Reverend Jones is a graduate of Loyola University, Andover Newton Theological School, and holds a Doctor of Ministry degree from Emory University and a Doctor of Philosophy degree from Drew University.

A pastor for twenty years, Reverend Jones was the founding minister of Beacon Light Baptist Church in New Orleans and the Senior Minister at Calvary Baptist Church, Chester, Penn.; Ebenezer Baptist Church, Boston, Mass.; and First Baptist Church, Randolph, Mass.. Throughout his pastoral ministry, Reverend Jones served on various religious and civic committees at the local and national level.

Dr. Jones currently teaches ethics and preaching at Andover Newton Theological School, and serves as a guest preacher and teacher at churches, schools, and conferences throughout the United States. His writings have been published in various journals, including *Leadership*, *Gospel Today*, *Pulpit Digest*, and *The African American Pulpit*, a quarterly preaching journal he co-founded in 1997.

Reverend Jones is the creator of an inspirational card collection called *Savoring Pace Life Lines* and www.savoringpace.com, a Web site which offers weekly reflections on cherishing life in a rushing world.

Dr. Jones is the author of *Rest in the Storm: Self-Care Strategies for Clergy and Other Caregivers* and *Addicted to Hurry: Spiritual Strategies for Slowing Down,* both published by Judson Press, and *The Jazz of Preaching: How to Preach with Great Freedom and Joy,* published by Abingdon Press.

Dr. Jones enjoys a leisure life of family, play, reading, walking and jogging, listening to music (especially jazz), playing computer and video games, and having new learning adventures every day.

You may learn more about Dr. Jones's speaking and writing at www.kirkbjones.com and www.brewseries.com.

Other Works
by Kirk Byron Jones

Morning B.R.E.W. Journal

Rest in the Storm:
Self-Care Strategies for Clergy and Other Caregivers

Addicted to Hurry:
Spiritual Strategies for Slowing Down

Savoring Pace Life Lines
(A fifty-card collection of inspirations designed to help
you slow down and relish life more)

The Jazz of Preaching:
How to Preach with Great Freedom and Joy

Also from Augsburg Books

". . . A soul-stirring devotional resource. Use Jones's words to jump-start your day with gusto and grace!"
— Frederic and Mary Ann Brussat, authors of
Spiritual Literacy: Reading the Sacred in Everyday Life

"God is inviting Christians into a deeper relationship. Disciples know the power of such sustained and intentional practices, and Kirk Jones speaks with conviction born out of his own experience and spiritual growth."
— Michael W. Foss, author of *Power Surge;*
A Servant's Manual; and *Real Faith for Real Life*

To order, call 1-800-328-4648
or go to www.augsburgbooks.com